Javier Mariscal Designing the New Spain

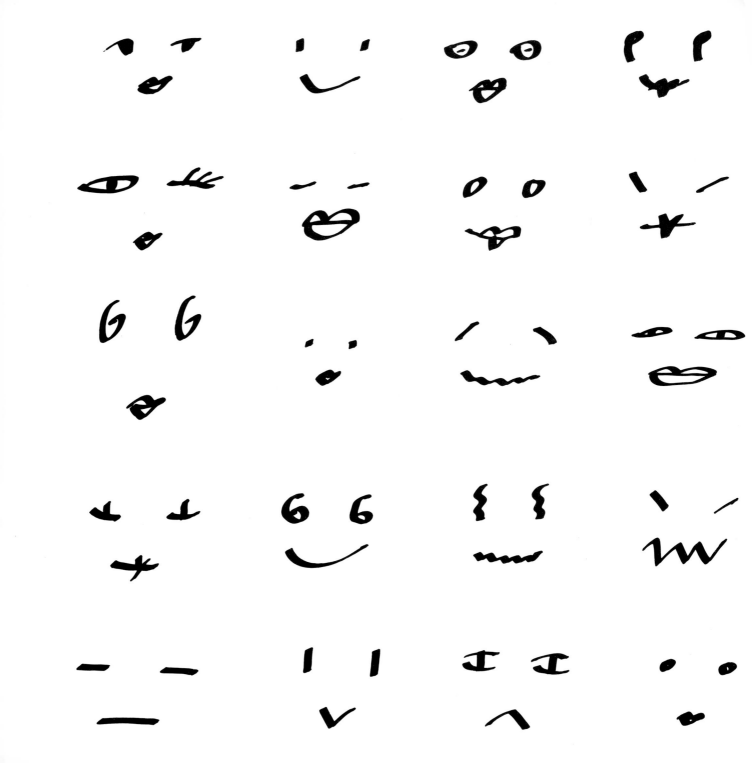

Javier Mariscal Designing the New Spain

A Blueprint Monograph
Published by Fourth Estate
and Wordsearch, London

RIZZOLI NEW YORK

By Emma Dent Coad

First published in
Great Britain in 1991 by
Fourth Estate Ltd,
289 Westbourne Grove,
London W11 2QA
in conjunction with *Blueprint*
magazine, 26 Cramer Street,
London W1M 3HE.

A catalogue record for this
book is available from the
British Library.

ISBN 1-87218-052-3
LCCCN 90-50820

Design: Martin Farran-Lee
Series Editor:
Arthur Valenzuela
Colour reproduction:
Fotographics Ltd.
UK/Hong Kong
Printed and bound
in Hong Kong

First published in the
United States of America in
1991 by Rizzoli International
Publications, Inc.,
300 Park Avenue South,
New York, New York 10010.

LCCCN 90-50820
ISBN 0-8478-1357-6

Photographic credits

David Banks 27; Enrico
Carrazoni 46, 69 and various
images from the catalogue
Cent Anys a BAR CEL ONA;
Carlos Errando 47; María
Espeus 4; Hector Ibáñez –
various images from the
catalogue *Cent Anys a
BAR CEL ONA*; Jordi Sarrà
70, 71, 73, 74/75, 77; Phil
Sayer – front cover; Marta
Sentís 42,43; Luís Sevillano
68; Rafael Vargas 78/79

Pages 2/3, 8/9, 12/13, 28/29,
40/41, 80/81, 96/97 contain
original drawings by Javier
Mariscal for this volume.

Acknowledgements

This book is based on a
number of conversations
with Javier Mariscal in late
1990. For their help and
encouragement, I would like
to thank: Gemma Beltrán,
David Blott, Juli Capella,
José-María Morillo,
Jordi Sarrà, Penny Sparke
and Judith Watt.

Blueprint Monographs

Ron Arad Restless Furniture
Deyan Sudjic
Nigel Coates
The City in Motion
Rick Poynor
Rei Kawakubo and
Commes des Garçons
Deyan Sudjic
Eva Jiricna Design in Exile
Martin Pawley
King and Miranda
The Poetry of the Machine
Hugh Aldersey-Williams

Contents

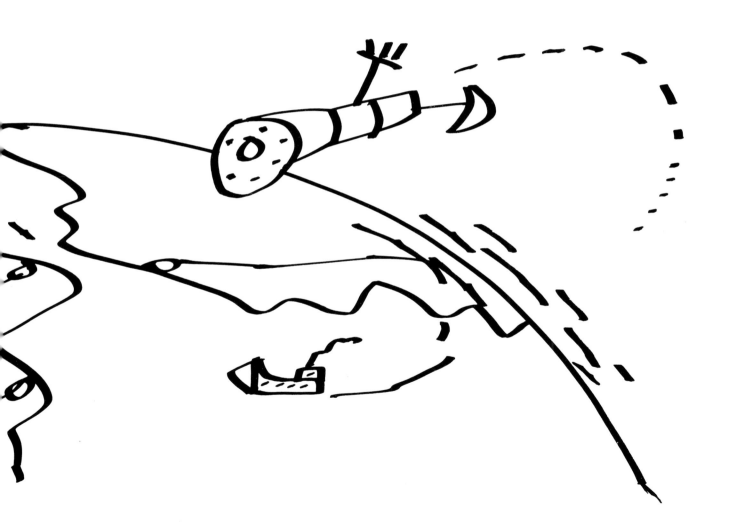

Mariscal's view of himself, surrounded by images of his life and work, drawing, 1983

It is interesting to consider whether in the future Javier Mariscal will be best known for his art or his design. He works feverishly in so many different areas – which to him are all "art" – that it is impossible to be confident about which is now or will be the most important aspect of his work. His paintings are included in some of the major collections of Spain, and his commissioned design work goes around the world. In his own country, he is equally well known for all the diverse forms which his work takes, from paintings to textiles, comics, china or his decorative input in bars. But for many, he will simply be "the Cobi man", responsible for the mascot of the Barcelona Olympics. Mariscal is easy-going enough to be content being associated forever with his famous chubby pink alter ego. With his ready smile and arms outstretched waiting to hug you, Cobi is very much Mariscal.

Beyond preaching goodwill, and good times to be had by all, Mariscal insists on being apolitical. He does, however, have firm ideas on the philosophy of the work at his studio: "What we do here is to create new languages and perfect languages which already exist. We play around with them and enrich them, giving them more shades of meaning. There is a feeling which I really like with this type of work – what it's doing is helping the world to understand itself better. When you create language you are giving it power, because you have more ways of meaning and expressing yourself."

"I often think that conflicts occur because of people not understanding each other. So our work tries to help people to understand themselves and each other, creating positive relationships. You can then understand other attitudes better; there is a bringing together of cultures and it helps people to get on better. You start out by thinking: 'How strange their language is! How do they think?' If you ask yourself these sorts of questions and learn to communicate better, you can have better relations with other people. To understand an Arab, for example, you must understand his religion, his language, why he talks so strangely, why he wears long robes, eats with his hands, prays so many times a day. If you can appreciate these things, then you will have a different perspective, with more subtleties, and it would be much more difficult to get into a fight with him….We believe in this type of language, using symbols which mean the same thing around the world."

One regular feature of Mariscal's work is his constant reworking of existing themes. Whether it is his Tío Pepe chair, his version of Las Meninas, a spontaneous "Japanese" interpretation of Barcelona in mixed media soy sauce and tofu on a restaurant tablecloth, or his very "Turkish" Kabul rug with images of modern kitchens within Islamic arches, Mariscal is simultaneously making fun of his subject, making it accessible, and creating a cultural empathy between the audience and the subject.

Mariscal is reluctant to take himself seriously. Approached by a fan in a bar, he is content to play second fiddle to an imaginary brother for half an hour ("No, no, I'm Carlos Mariscal – Javier is taller than me…"). During very Spanish philosophical discussions about design, he never hesitates to bring matters down to earth with a subtle joke or an earthy story. Characteristically, Mariscal expresses himself with a deceptive simplicity capable of being understood at many levels, and in many cultures. He uses symbols, events and icons that are internationally comprehensible. Cobi has become a universal symbol, reproduced in windows and shops from London to Tokyo. It has the tang of Barcelona's unique identity, not the bland anonimity of a Coca-Cola logo. Mariscal synthesises cultures and experiences in a way that celebrates diversity.

Valencia to Barcelona

Few designers can have had an early career which so closely reflected the transformations which shaped the society in which they lived and worked. Javier Mariscal has gone from penniless art school drop-out to international celebrity in the course of a single decade. Equally, few designers have been so ready to present an utterly unassuming face to the world. Despite his status as unofficial national spokesman for the new Spain, and his prolific talent, Mariscal portrays himself as an entertainer, content to play the clown.

At the beginning of the 1950s, when Mariscal was born, Spain was one of the poorest countries in Europe, its economy in ruins and its cultural life stultified by more than a decade of fascist rule under the dictator General Francisco Franco. But, as Mariscal reached maturity, the Franco years were coming to an end, and Spain began to emerge as an important creative centre. The simultaneous staging of the 25th Olympic Games in Barcelona and the Universal Exposition in Seville in 1992 marks the passage of a former cultural backwater into a social and economic force, as well as a decisive shift in the political and social geography of Europe towards the Mediterranean. For Mariscal himself, the Games brought universal recognition for at least one piece of his work – Cobi, the official Olympic mascot.

On the face of it, Mariscal's cubist cartoon dog might be regarded as simply a frivolous joke. Yet it is inconceivable that any other country could have adopted such a knowingly subversive icon for so highly charged an international event.

Of course no designer could be said to be responsible for all the changes in the cultural climate of a country of 40 million people. But for many, Mariscal's work has come to symbolise Spain's newly acquired position at the centre of the European stage. Not quite a painter, not quite a designer, Mariscal has given the new Spain a graphic signature for its rebirth as an open society, no longer trapped by the oppressive weight of its traditions.

Since the mid 1970s Mariscal's endless creativity has poured out a constant stream of logotypes, paintings, objects, cartoons and

The future Olympic mascot, Cobi, in an early sketch, 1988

**Cobi Sobrevolando
Barcelona [Cobi Flying
Over Barcelona], 1988**

occasionally furniture and buildings. Yet when he staged his first exhibition in a shabby Barcelona arts centre in 1977, he didn't even have the price of a cup of coffee. He now runs a studio in Poble Nou, steering a path between creative chaos and the professional organisation needed to serve mainstream commercial clients from IBM to Coca-Cola, from Japan to Germany. And he is a highly visible celebrity, treated with suspicion by some, but popularly seen as at least in part responsible for Barcelona's new-found international status.

Mariscal's career as a designer has been shaped by his experience of two very different Spanish cities: provincial Valencia, where he was born, and cosmopolitan Barcelona, where he has lived since his days as a student. The complex, uneasy relationship between the two cities is the key to understanding Mariscal's work, and provides a revealing insight into the nature of the modern Spanish state. The rivalry is counterbalanced by a sneaking sympathy between two cities, both marginalised in recent history by the chauvinistic dominance of the national capital, Madrid.

Mariscal's progress northward from Valencia was a rite of passage. Valencia, Spain's third city, left an indelible stamp on his aesthetic sensibilities in his early years. He moved to Barcelona in his teens, rapidly making a mark in the much larger city.

In his early days in Barcelona, Mariscal's life centred on the dusty cafés and bars of the Barrio Gótico (this was before Barcelona's nightlife had been transformed by high design) and on the beaches along the coast, where summers drifted lazily by through a cloud of marijuana and rock music.

Both Barcelona and Valencia are ports, and both share the Catalan language, but they have had very different histories. Valencia still bears traces of its Moorish heritage. Its core is a medieval tangle of twisting lanes; its outskirts are studded with villas and tower blocks. It's a hedonistic place whose lush climate dulls the sharp edges of the daily struggle for existence. Barcelona on the other hand – despite its blue skies – is Spain's industrial heartland, with its banks and factories. It is a northern city in a southern country. Physically, it is dominated by the rationalist grid of its nineteenth-century plan.

The real antagonism which exists between Barcelona and Madrid mirrors the relationship between Milan and Rome. Barcelona, like Milan, is a place where people may spend late nights in the bars and restaurants, but still get on with their work the next morning. There are fewer bureaucrats and more industrialists.

When Javier Mariscal was born in 1950, the fourth son of a moderately prosperous doctor with eleven children, Spain, as far as the rest of Europe was concerned, was still the dark house at the end of the street with the bodies buried in the garden. Nothing much had been heard from the inhabitants since the commotion of the civil war.

General Franco had maintained his stranglehold on the country for nearly a dozen years, and the corporatist policies which emanated from Madrid ensured the continuing isolation of his subjects. Imports were heavily discouraged by tariff walls built to protect state-run monopolies from more efficient competitors. Moreover, the Caudillo was equally determined to insulate Spain from subversive cultural influences abroad. Before mass tourism began to take off in the early 1960s, only a few determined travellers had managed to penetrate its frontiers. The economy, untouched by consumer-driven demand, was primitive. The car industry for example, now as big as Great Britain's, was all but non-existent in the 1950s, producing a limited range of outmoded Fiats. What up-to-date factories there were, depended on licensing agreements with foreign manufacturers, and a major industry developed around copying foreign goods – innovation was officially discouraged as subversive.

After Portugal, Spain's living standards during this period were, by a wide margin, the lowest in Western Europe. Much of the country remained frozen in a pre-industrial peasant economy, and huge numbers of Spaniards moved north to France, Germany and Britain in search of work. Refrigerators and television sets were still very rare, let alone private cars. Industrial design in this context was scarcely

An angelic Mariscal, at his first holy communion, 1957

relevant. There was neither the market nor the potential to make sophisticated consumer goods. As a cultural activity, design was highly suspect – the avant-garde was identified with the Republicans and dissident Catalan nationalists. Economically, industrial design had little role to play, given the backward state of Spanish industry and scarcity of imports with which to compete. But there was still a vigorous artisan tradition of craft workshops and hand-made objects, and it was this that provided the foundation for the explosion of interest in Spanish design in the 1980s. Latterly, the strong sense of regional identity of a traditional society seems increasingly attractive in the context of the homogenised world of the modern industrial metropolis, and it is that which Spain now offers, underpinning its new-found modernity.

Looking back at the photographs of Mariscal's first communion in his little naval uniform and white gloves, you get the poignant sense of a vanished world that feels as far removed from the present day as a Velázquez court portrait. Stiff and formal, he seems trapped in the musty solemn embrace of a permanent Sunday. Indeed, at that time, Spain was still a country in which the Guardia Civil arrested women for wearing bikinis, or tourists who made the mistake of kissing in public.

Despite its charm as a Mediterranean city, the recent history of Valencia has been extraordinarily violent. Even before the outbreak of the civil war, political arson and even killings were common. After the Fascists began the rebellion against the Republican government, Valencia remained a Republican stronghold for a year after after the fall of Madrid, and it was here that the die-hard anti-Fascists made their last stand in 1939.

In the aftermath of the Civil War, Valencia was far from being Franco's favourite city. There was a settling of old scores and, like Barcelona, Valencia suffered under a policy of deliberate economic neglect. The little investment there was in the Spanish economy was directed towards what the Madrid government saw as more deserving cases. However, Franco's authoritarianism could never entirely wipe out the exuberance of the older Spain.

Castillo de Rafa, Barcelona (opposite). Fantastic architecture and a designer interior, including some Mariscal furniture. From *Historias de Garriris*, 1986

Valencia felt a little like California even then. A place of open skies and wide beaches, orange groves and flowers, irrigation had made the region an oasis in the middle of semi-arid Spain. Houses were cheap, if simple, and the sunshine allowed people to spend most of the year outside. "I love the city, it has a real culture of its own, and a distinctive architecture of patios, gardens and stone encrusted with vegetation," Mariscal says now. "It isn't like England, where you build a house, lay out a garden, put up a wall, paint it every year and cut the grass. When Valencians build a house, they put up some cement blocks, then they run out of money and stop building. Then, when they're doing a bit better, they put in a garden, and some geraniums. But it's always provisional – nothing is ever permanent."

Mariscal grew up just as two decades of self-imposed Spanish isolation began to lift. The United States Air Force arrived in the 1950s, when Franco signed an agreement with Eisenhower to allow US air-bases on Spanish soil. The Americans brought Elvis and Coca-Cola with them, adding yet another overlay to what was already an extraordinarily lurid cultural mix. Despite a repressive government, censorship and a conservative moral climate, the 1960s were a far from dreary time to be a teenager in Spain. "Abroad there is a myth that the Franco period was nothing but misery. It's true as far as ideas and formal liberties go but, nonetheless, the bars never closed, coffee, cognac, wine and cigarettes were incredibly cheap, and drugs were really easy to get hold of," says Mariscal, who has always believed in having as good a time as possible.

Valencia had been a caliphate at the time of the Moorish occupation of Spain and, 500 years later, North African customs still linger. Even today, you can see vivid reminders of the Moors in the white plaster architecture, and in the villages inland where, customarily, women do not eat with their husbands. The men are masters in their houses; the women are there to serve them. "It has a very African feeling. The Arabs were here for a long time, and they left behind a tradition of building in plaster. You can do lots of things with it –

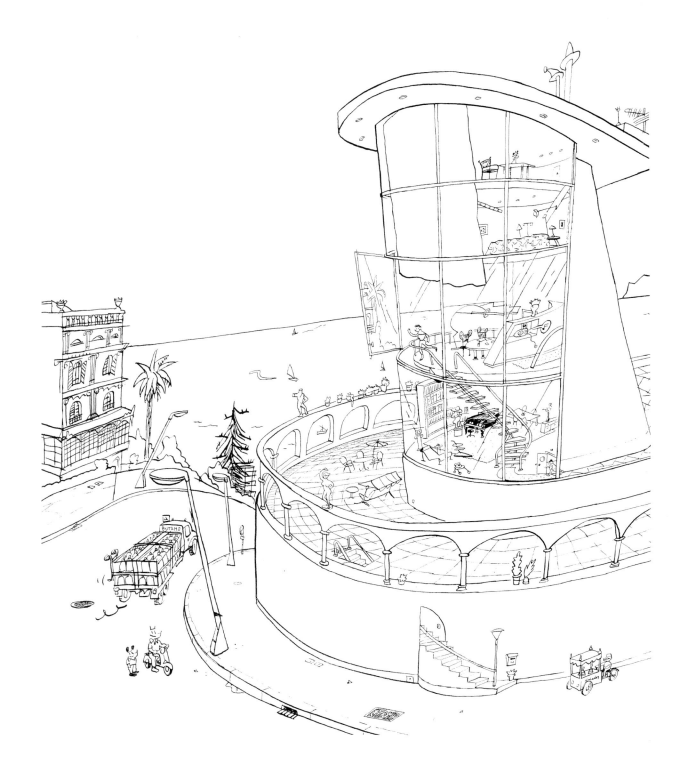

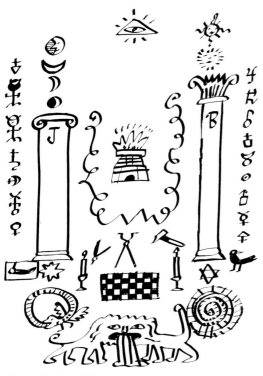

Mariscal designed the graphics for the nightclub Las Torres de Ávila, 1990

you can create a wonderful palace in no time at all, but it just falls apart after a while." Even Valencia's medieval quarter behind the cathedral, with its narrow winding streets and tall buildings has a ramshackle quality. Very little attempt is made to stop its historic buildings crumbling to dust. "It's a very Valencian approach", says Mariscal. "They like to do things that are quick and easy – to have some fun, and then move on to something else. They would get totally bored trying to do something long term like staging the Olympics the way that Barcelona has done. They would rather have something new than something old, even if it's fifteenth century. They just knock old buildings down."

Mariscal is keenly aware of Valencia's past. Together with Catalonia, Ibiza and the other Balearic Islands, the city of Valencia and its surrounding province was once part of Aragón – a medieval kingdom which had been greatly influenced by France to the north as well as by Madrid. "The concept is of the Arabs having conquered Spain in a single battle, but it wasn't really like that. It was more at the level of the village people who changed their way of life very slowly under the influence of really very few people of the Arab race. To say that the Arabs conquered Spain would be like saying that the Americans had invaded us in the late twentieth century. Of course we are being Americanised. Like all countries, we have Madonna, we have supermarkets and Fords, motorways and Coca-Cola, but it's much more complex than calling it "an invasion". It's a question of people taking on elements of different cultures that seem attractive, and adopting them as their own."

Mariscal's own work has the apparently effortless quality of Valencian architecture to the extent that some critics write him off as "facile". He draws with an easy fluency, his distinctive ink line deftly sketching cartoons that merge into paintings with a florid colour sense that seems to come straight from his home town. But there is an intensity to the colour and line that makes him anything but superficial.

Back in 1957, Valencia's river had a more than usually destructive flood which left large parts of the city in ruins. The drive to rebuild the city in its aftermath left an abiding mark on Mariscal's imagination, and a fascination for memories from that period. "The river flooded a large part of the city, and once everything had been cleaned up, they had to do a lot of new building. There is a whole school of new bars and shops from that time with a very distinctive style. As it was 1958, everything was made from Formica and used fluorescent colours. This went down very well in Valencia, where there is a great feeling for loud colours. Valencians would rather paint their houses swimming-pool green than brown – a Valencian woman would rather paint her lips bright scarlet and nails electric pink, rather than violet. It's a bit like Hollywood."

This sense of colour certainly informs Mariscal's own work, and is based on a sensibility that sounds very much like the interest in the banal imagery of neighbourhood bars, and anonymous, unselfconscious design that fuelled Memphis, the Milanese group. Indeed, twenty years later, Mariscal was able to feel an immediate rapport with Ettore Sottsass when he asked him to do some work for the Memphis collection.

America, of course, was Mariscal's other youthful obsession. He discovered Levi jeans and Frank Zappa in his teens. He grew his hair long, started to listen to Jimi Hendrix, the Doors and Dylan, and toured the rock festivals of Europe. And of course he started to see the outpouring of West Coast comics from Robert Crumb and others who translated the comic-strip character from mainstream to outlaw. Crumb, at that time, was still a part of what used to be called "The Underground". It's a description that, given Franco's continuing presence, could much more appropriately be applied to the more enterprising end of the spectrum of Spanish cultural life at that time.

These two strands of the day-glo fifties and alternative Americana left Mariscal with a ready-made personal visual vocabulary when, in 1971, he moved to Barcelona to study graphic design at the Escuela Elisava, the city's first private design school, which opened at the start of the 1960s. The course itself left Mariscal entirely unimpressed, but

**"Un Diumenche pel Matí",
published in *A Valencia*
magazine, 1975. Mariscal
was still under the
influence of the West
Coast underground**

Mariscal's impression of Olympic Barcelona, with revolving cable-cars transferring passengers between sites

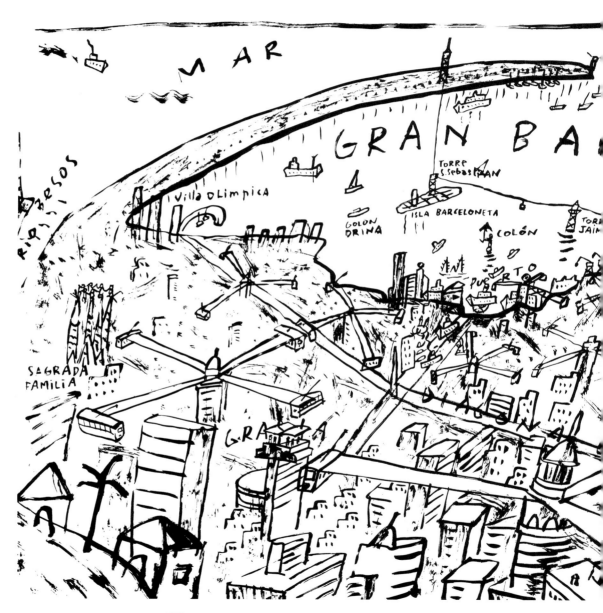

Barcelona turned out to be the making of the young designer. Valencians may speak a version of Catalan, but their day-to-day life is very different from that of the average Barcelonés. "People are much less organised back in Valencia," says Mariscal, who remains somewhat ambiguous about his new home.

Nevertheless, success in Barcelona came easily. A constant stream of drawings, sketches and designs poured out of his pen, the product of an overheated and prolific imagination. It was simple force of circumstance that pushed him in the direction of comic strips. "If I'd had more money I'd have made films, but the easiest thing at the time was to get some Chinese ink and white paper and make photocopies – the easiest way to tell a story was through comics." As a student Mariscal lived in the Barrio Gótico of Barcelona's old town. He was there in time to see the city waking from the torpor of the late Franco era, though there was still enough lingering repression in the air for his cartoons to cause a stir and force him to leave for the less pressured atmosphere of Ibiza for a while.

At the same time that Mariscal was beginning to make a name for himself as a bright young talent, Spain itself was changing. The country's economy was expanding rapidly, and it began to enjoy an increasingly international reputation as a cultural force. This in turn expanded Mariscal's own opportunities. He was quickly a big fish in what was becoming a bigger and bigger pond. From producing home-made strip cartoons, Mariscal was perfectly positioned when the fledgling furniture companies started looking for new and interesting designs from home-grown talent.

The years since Franco died have been kind to Barcelona – it is Spain's second city only when measured by the size of its population. Its vitality and optimism sometimes make even Madrid seem introverted and provincial by comparison. More to the point, Barcelona is the capital of Catalonia, a nation with its own language and traditions, of a size and economic muscle that would outstrip fully fledged members of the United Nations such as Denmark. Even at the

"Mediterraneo con
Avión", sketch for the
centre page of *Neón
de Suro*, 1976

turn of the century, Barcelona's intellectuals and painters were more
interested in Paris and London than in Madrid. Picasso's favourite café,
the Quatre Gats, advertised itself as "a place for lovers of the north".

The liberating influence of democratic government in Madrid gave
Barcelona substantial autonomy and literally transformed Catalonia.
Catalan, a forbidden language under Franco, began to replace
Castillian in the city's streets, and Barcelona seized economic and
cultural leadership. The most important driving factor was Spain's entry
into the European Economic Community, a move that has had huge
repercussions for Spanish industry. In the run-up to membership, the
Madrid government took a whole range of steps to encourage

The Trampolín chair, designed in collaboration with Pepe Cortés in 1986 and produced by Akaba Lasarte (Guipúzcoa)

industrialists to gear up to producing goods sophisticated enough to survive in the face of competition from the wider European market.

The tariff walls were coming down, and if the old monopolies had not broadened their product ranges they would have gone the same way as the East German corporations a decade later. Design was seen as an important part of the equation, and substantial government subsidies were poured into schemes which encouraged manufacturers to use and promote young Spanish designers effectively. One result of this drive was the mushrooming of Spanish design magazines, underwritten in part by subsidies, which helped to promote designers such as Mariscal.

Of course all this effort only acheived the success that it did because it coincided with a genuine eruption of creative talent, first in Barcelona's bars and nightclubs, then in the wider economy outside. In the process, Barcelona became a blend of London from the Swinging Sixties, and Milan as a design centre.

The idea of Barcelona establishing itself as a rival capital of design is by no means a far-fetched idea. There are many similarities between Barcelona in its present state – full of small workshops, on the point of emerging from a craft tradition – and the Milan of the 1950s.

The old Barcelona, a port city of claustrophobic streets contained within thick walls and bisected by the *ramblas*, remains miraculously intact. Surrounding it are the grids of nineteenth-century planners, who transformed the city in its industrial heyday. The streets are still full of the sumptuous and often outlandish houses built by affluent industrialists in a style which is unique in its lack of restraint. The new European city that is now emerging retains some of the quirkiness of that era, for all its newly discovered international outlook. Mariscal helped to establish Barcelona's reputation as a city brimming with energy . His BAR CEL ONA design, later adopted by the city as part of its deliberate programme of image-building, follows in the steps of Milton Glazer's famous I ♥ NY campaign and helped to dispel the idea of Spain as an outpost of the third world. Barcelona, through

Early drawing for the Bar Cel Ona [bar/sky/wave] poster (above), 1979. Mariscal with his regular collaborator, industrial designer Pepe Cortés (opposite)

Mariscal's eye, became: Bar [bar], Cel [sky] and Ona [wave].

The seal on Barcelona's international stature was set by its selection for the 1992 Olympics. Mariscal has played a large role in creating a graphic identity for the games. But just as Barcelona now has to cope with the stresses of its own success as it faces up to the prospect of a wave of international tourists, vertiginous property price-increases and sterile new hotels, so Mariscal himself has to deal with the problems of turning his fertile creative imagination into a business. "I used to have to do everything: answer the phone, meet with the client, do the invoices, think about the work, *do* it, wrap it up, deliver it on the motorbike, collect payment. Now we have a receptionist, secretary, graphic artists, computer link-up, messenger, finance director, accountants and lawyer." The point of all this organisaton is to make Mariscal's life easier, and to give him the time to do more elaborate work. Predictably, things have not turned out quite as clear-cut as Mariscal had hoped: "Of course sometimes I get fed up with it all. Goodness and happiness cannot exist without feeling bad sometimes. Sometimes I think about my studio: 'I've been here a year – everyone's taking money and putting nothing in.' But after two weeks it's all over and everything's fine. Then I think: 'Without these people here, we couldn't do anything. They're so clever, so kind. They put so much love in.' Both things are real and true."

A mouse's-eye view

Piker and Fermín, Los Garriris, clear their throats at the start of an adventure

The droll El Señor del Caballito, which first appeared in 1970

Bored by conventional graphic design, Mariscal began earning a precarious living as a comic-strip artist while he was still as student at the Elisava school in Barcelona. It was a spontaneous medium that came easily to him, and it turned out to be the starting point for all of his other work in both a literal and stylistic sense. Not only does Mariscal transform his more successful cartoons into three-dimensional objects, he also uses the narrative and graphic techniques of the strip cartoon as the basis for designing furniture and interiors. According to the Barcelona furniture designer Carlos Riart: "Mariscal converts all the little cartoons that pass through his head into objects. It's as if you opened up a comic and found all the people and objects made real – like a sweet dream." Mariscal himself has a strictly limited attention span. He is easily distracted. Like his cartoon characters, with whom he has much in common, Mariscal lives for the moment.

During the 1960s, Mariscal became deeply involved in the counter-culture. He lived in a commune, experimented with LSD and grew his hair – though he eventually cut it to please his mother. He also did the circuit of European rock festivals, in the process absorbing the atmosphere of moral and sexual freedom, a sharp contrast to the conventional values prevalent in Spain in general, and to the world of his deeply conservative parents in particular. He kept up a steady stream of postcards to his ten siblings at home, and these drawings were his first foray into the world of cartoons.

In Spain, as in France and Japan, the comic strip has a much more culturally respectable image than it does in Britain. There is a long tradition of strips, which have become a highly evolved form in Spain. There are comics aimed at virtually every age group and taste, from "graphic novels" as they are called by enthusiasts, to blood-thirsty westerns and pornographic exotica. It's a tradition that grew out of the popularity of picture novels, and their specifically Catalan form, *aucas*, satirical vignettes with abbreviated story-lines, which developed at the turn of the century.

Barcelona, for long a centre for publishing and graphic art, is now

El Señor del Caballito in an early adventure, unpublished, 1970

the comic-strip capital at least of Spain, if not the whole of Europe. It is full of publishing houses which specialise in this much misunderstood minor art. There is such a concentration of graphic artists working on comic strips in Barcelona that even the British newspaper industry beats a path to their door, content to supply its own texts to fill the bubbles drawn by Spaniards without even the most limited English.

Along with some fellow students, and friends from outside the school, following a pattern set by the strips from San Francisco, Mariscal published *El Rrollo Enmascarado* [Masked Tedium], a comic that had vaguely underground inclinations. After he left Elisava, drawing, publishing and selling the strips became a full-time occupation: "I started with comics because it was the easiest thing to do when I was young. I wasn't going to do mainstream graphics, and at the time I thought painting was very bourgeois, that it was only for people with money, and I didn't want to dedicate my work to these people. Distribution was easy: we photocopied the strips and sold them on the streets – you get instant feed-back this way."

Mariscal did work for some more conventional publications. He produced a strip called *El Señor del Caballito* [The Man with the Little Horse], for a Christian Democrat magazine, which consisted of mainly visual and graphic jokes. Its inspirations were more Steinberg and Folon than The Fabulous Furry Freak Brothers. Mariscal's economical line drawings struck a consciously arty tone, putting figures in geometric landscapes and composing frames for their formal impact, rather than accepting the unpretentious tradition of the authentic strip; it was as if he wasn't quite ready to relinquish the last vestiges of graphic respectability yet. Mariscal's diminutive horseman found himself pursued by giant arrows, caught up in a Mondrian painting and taking a tour around Manhattan with very little in the way of dialogue.

But his main outlet was at the opposite side of the political spectrum. Barcelona had a number of underground magazines during the last years of the Franco regime, and Mariscal worked for several of

Los Garriris from *Star*, no. 21, 1976. Piker gives Fermín a lift in his curious automobile with sidecar

them, in particular for *Purita*, *A la Calle*, and *El Sidecar*. Many of them followed the American comic formula – worked out ten years earlier and by now looking a little tired – fairly closely, with story-lines based on drug-related fantasies and sexual excess. However, Mariscal's own cartoons, even those dealing with sex, have a charm and innocence which transcends the genre, more ribald Donald Duck than decadent Fritz the Cat. Mariscal created a whole cast of characters that appeared time and time again, skipping between strips and magazines. An early comic was *Una Chica Desenvuelta* [A Wayward Girl], which chronicled the life of a modern Barcelona girl going to wild parties, wearing outrageous clothes and having a good time. Other characters were one-offs, gently satirising comfortable Barcelona attitudes and lifestyles, though avoiding serious social comment (Mariscal has never been politically active).

Mariscal's graphic technique was clearly influenced by the American strips. Like Robert Crumb, Mariscal took the conventions of an entirely unchallenging graphic form and turned them around to highly subversive effect. At first he made much of animating inanimate objects. He drew palm trees with faces, sprouting arms with gloved hands and gave them feet with little open-toed sandals. But unlike Crumb, Mariscal always had a fluency and a sense of space and openness in his strips. Drugs were never allowed to dominate them, and the paranoia of psychedelia was kept at bay. As time went by, he escaped from the influence of American models and established his own distinctive style. The frames are not heavily boxed in, or crammed with detail. Rather, they have an allusiveness that is much closer to art than most strips can achieve. In the early days, to keep costs down, he had to stick to black and white, a fact which gave his work its immediacy. There is little use of tone; instead his strong, but fractured lines, and deep black shadows bring the flat shapes to life. Words are integrated with the images, rather than kept separate, though story lines have never been that strong a part of Mariscal's strips.

By 1975, Barcelona's underground press was having a harder time

Los Garriris (top) on the cover of *El Sidecar*, 1976. Una Chica Desenvuelta (above) on the cover of *El Víbora* summer special, 1984

Los Garriris go fishing and catch a dog (Julián) in *El Víbora*, no. 32-33, 1981

of it, in the face of Franco's last gasp. Slow to realise that they were far from being as innocuous as they looked, the censors were reading the strips at last and did not like what they found. Like many Spanish hippies, Mariscal moved to Ibiza, where restrictions were not so strictly enforced as on the mainland. He stayed two years, all the while drawing and enjoying the sybaritic hippy lifestyle to the full. It was on his return that he conceived his first exhibition, *Gran Hotel*, after which cartoons became only one of many forms of expression open to him.

It was during this period that *Los Garriris* made their first appearance in *De Quommic* in 1974 . The strip was Mariscal's most fully worked out comic creation, a picaresque story of Barcelona life, in which he himself played a prominent role. Mariscal has hinted that the two heroes, Piker and Fermín, respectively a counter-cultural mouse and a hound, represent himself and his friend Sefer Pastor when they first came to Barcelona (Mariscal is the mouse): two wide-eyed strangers in a big, bad city. Their friends are the glamorous Chincheta and Julián, "El Perro Pescador" [The Fishing Dog, which also has some of Mariscal's characteristics]. They lead a cast of hundreds through adventures around the beaches, bars, clubs, and parties of Barcelona. There is a lot of love interest. To paraphrase Andy Robinson and Niclas Dünebacke's analysis of the Garriri lifestyle: never before in the history of the cartoon had two creatures downed as many rum-and-cokes, chatted up so many women, or gone for so many spins on a Vespa. Los Garriris tour the starlit freeways of an exotic metropolis studded with bullet-shaped hot pink gas stations, Cadillac Eldorados and hill-top villas. Mariscal alternately renders their surroundings in loving detail, or quickly scratches his characters into life with a few spikey lines that twitch with energy. The Garriris established themselves in *El Víbora* – a satire and soft-porn magazine of the late seventies, and continued to appear at least once a year until very recently. Julián was eventually immortalised in cast aluminium by Fernando Amat for his shop Vinçon.

Mariscal sees the comic as the perfect medium for him: "They are so concentrated. With just a few lines you have to give an idea of time,

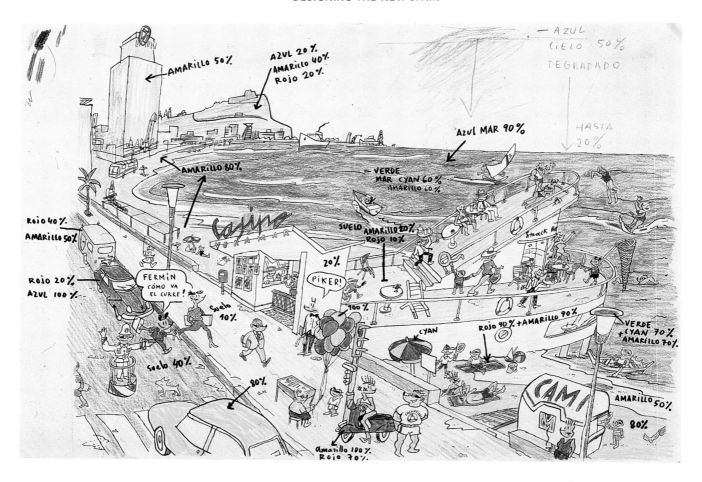

"Este Verano te vas a Enamorar" [This Summer You're Going to Fall in Love] – Proof of a cover for *El Víbora*, 1981

rhythm, atmosphere – you can explain with the least possible effort that the moon is over the sea on a summer's night, and that there are two lovers in a car."

His interest in comics derives from the very Valencian attitude of *día, día* – living for today. He doesn't plan, and is not interested in analysing his past performance. He also likes his work to have great diffusion, and a comic is the perfect medium for this: it's cheap and accessible. His current interest in rap music is another manifestation of this attitude, and goes back to his childhood when he used to "rap" at

A party scene from *El Víbora*, no. 56-57, 1984, provokes two very different reactions from guests: "What a Party!", versus "I hate people! I hate parties!" from the man writhing on the bed

home. There was always music at home, but as he couldn't sing he would talk through songs, often improvising in staccato bursts of words. He was often asked to do it without changing the words, but found it impossible. "If say, it was a love song and I knew my sister was in love with a boy, I used to change the song to include their names and the problems they were going through. I like rap now because it's immediate, very *de la calle* [street], very free, vital, fresh and energetic. This is why I like it, and this is how I like my work to be," asserts Mariscal. What his cartoons did for him in the long term was to ensure a

In "La Luna Mora"
[Moorish Moon] 1978, Los
Garriris dive in to save the
moon, which they believe
has fallen into the sea.
They imagine a passing
ship transporting the
moon to a distant port

In "Una Historia Muy
Negra" [A Very Black
Story] 1976, an anxiety-
ridden Piker comes to
the conclusion:
"I'm going to die"

strong popular following, something that few designers can ever achieve, but a factor which has always been part of Mariscal's success. Mariscal's constituency is not limited to the hermetic world of design. Rather, it has a genuinely popular touch – not élitist, but not talking down to people either.

Writing in *De Diseño* in 1986, Antoni Marí commented on the number of contemporary buildings and recognisable pieces of furniture that Mariscal had incorporated into his cartoons – his own, and that of others. His cartoon characters certainly live in the same sophisticated world as Mariscal, and enjoy the same things: the beach, women, music, dancing, drinking, making love and, above all, the sun. Mariscal's cartoons, drawings and paintings are all summer scenes; it is *the* time of year for him – the time to fall in love.

Mariscal has great *cariño* [affection] for the human race; this is evident in the way that he treats the minutiae of everyday life in his drawings. In one strip, La Chica Desenvuelta is phoned by her boyfriend for a date. The story, *¡No sé qué ponerme!* [I Don't Know What to Wear] goes through the girl's agonising search through her wardrobe for something suitable, until she goes out in a wild outfit with nothing matching, not even the shoes. This was animated for the title sequence of a TV fashion programme in 1986. In others, electric kitchen equipment takes on a life of its own: whizzing, buzzing, or flying around the room, dragging plug and leads behind them.

Behind Mariscal's melancholy, rather weary clown façade, he has a dead-pan humour which is sometimes so subtle that it is difficult to catch. "Why are you so serious, when I'm talking nonsense?"

Fishing alongside a band of robbers (Los Golfos Apanadores), Fermín tries to lure the rather un-cooperative lobsters and prawns with music, *El Vibora*, no. 91, 1987

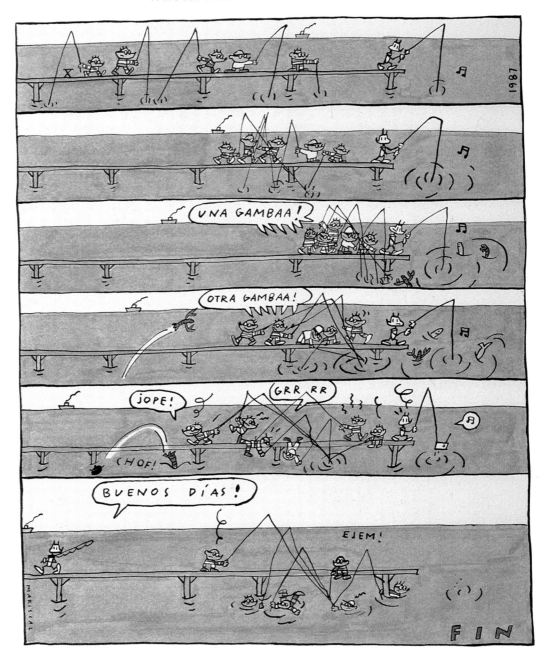

Chapter Three

Poster for the exhibition
Gran Hotel, 1977 (top);
reception area in the
Gran Hotel (above);
interior of the Decorapart
exhibition (opposite) at
Detrás Vinçon, 1978

SPACES AND OBJECTS

Mariscal's passionate love affair with the 1950s was finally consumated in 1977, when, newly returned from his self-imposed exile on the island of Ibiza, he decided to put on a sprawling installation-cum-exhibition encompassing the whole range of his work. He chose the Mec-Mec Gallery, a shabby back-street arts centre in Barcelona as the venue for *Gran Hotel*, a cinematic exploration of Mariscal's view of the past. With a group of friends, Mariscal created an imaginary 1950s hotel within the gallery, with different areas transformed into a reception, bar, lounge, bedroom and bathroom. Rather than hang isolated pictures on walls, Mariscal created an episodic evocation of banal modernity in affectionate parody of the faded glamour of the recent past. It was an amateur affair, done on a shoe-string with borrowed money – playful, but powerful all the same. Junk-shop radios, TVs and fifties' furniture – some of it re-upholstered to his own design – were the backdrop to his exhibition of graphics, video, strip cartoons, posters and little papier mâché sculptures of his cartoon characters. Their surprisingly complete world even extended as far as specially drawn book matches. Walls were painted with 1950s motifs and reclaimed lights from the period provided illumination. The "reception" sold T-shirts, badges and a variety of decorative objects to recover some of the costs. This was the first explosion of Mariscal's universe, a world in which he had his hand in everything; the show also provided a showcase for the results of his early excursions into three dimensions.

Gran Hotel's popular success put Mariscal on the map in Barcelona. His timing was perfect. It was the year after Franco's death, and the press and public were looking for signs of a more optimistic future, perhaps even – though they didn't know it yet – a new image for a more stylish Spain after the dowdy austerity of authoritarianism. The exhibit also signalled an important new direction for Mariscal, provided expression for some of his wilder fantasies and gave him the opportunity to see some of them manufactured. Mariscal's outlandish prototypes for furniture and lighting attracted considerable attention from Spanish manufacturers who were wondering where their future

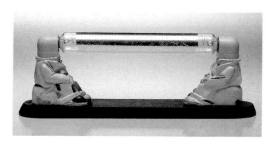

**Amigos Telepáticos
[Telepathic Friends] lamp
prototype, made by
Pep Molins and Eduardo
Pastor, 1978**

lay. Mariscal seemed to offer useful pointers: he was avant-garde, but he was popular too. In one seminal piece, a ceramic lamp, called *Amigos Telepáticos* [Telepathic Friends], two small figures face each other on chairs. Their heads consist of fluorescent bulb fixtures, and a bulb joins the two at the head. Inexplicably, this ingenious and quirky idea has yet to be manufactured. The prototype is in a private collection, as are many other designs regarded as potentially important pieces of art rather than market failures. Even if they looked wilful and less-than-serious, they had the easy confidence of someone who knows where he is going.

Mariscal's designs still had a cartoon quality to them. His lights and chairs were props from his strip cartoons. Their sensibility was closer to the jokey surrealism of contemporary English teapots with little Mickey Mouse feet than anything else. In as far as he thought about it at all, Mariscal's view of design was intuitive. The onslaught on the conventional good taste of the modern movement still seemed fresh. The discovery of the charm of kitsch had not yet gone stale. And Mariscal was content to go on mining these still rich seams.

Mariscal's first real commission for an interior was in 1978 on Merbeyé, one of the forerunners of Barcelona's avalanche of fashionable bars. And predictably, perhaps, it took the form of a cartoon brought to life. Mariscal was never shy of admitting that his technical and organisational skills were limited, and for all such projects he relied on one or another of a group of collaborators. Their different emphases and inputs has left a clear mark. They show the different twists and turns in Mariscal's evolution from simple comic strips. Mariscal was asked to collaborate on Merbeyé by Fernando Amat, owner of the Vinçon shop and the man who has been at the centre of Barcelona's emergence as a significant force in design. It was Amat who had first received the commission to design Merbeyé's interiors.

Mariscal's background is not as a manipulator of space, but even here, his work is not simply a matter of choosing colours and patterns as a decorator. Merbeyé displays Mariscal's interest in mechanisms and movement, and in design with more depth than superficial style. The most striking features of the bar are its large rotating fans, painted in a 1950s-inspired pattern, but more pointedly, they slice through two steel columns that appear to hold up the roof. Two cartoons that Mariscal drew at the time tell the story. The first, *Falta de Previsión* [Lack of Forethought], shows Mariscal up a ladder making the unwelcome discovery that he has put the fans too close to the columns. Meanwhile, Amat stands at the bottom of the ladder handing up a saw, so that Mariscal can chop out a section to allow the blades of the fan to to rotate freely. It's a strong visual gag. But in the flesh the effect is more mesmerising than humorous. The second cartoon, *Hubo Problemas con las Medidas* [We had Problems with the Measurements] is a sketch of the bar with various problems pointed out: "twisted angles, badly finished paintwork, cork (not wood) too short, wrong measurements, bad use of the Colilla lamp" and the like.

Bar Duplex, in Valencia, the best known of Mariscal's early interiors, was another collaboration, this time with Fernando Salas and is much closer to the high-design bars that Barcelona architects were starting to turn out at the time. It recycles 1950s modernism as a decorative style. The large two-storey bar had a mezzanine with an organic curving profile that seems to pre-empt the neo-constructivism of Zaha Hadid or Rem Koolhaas. A raised floor continued the curves, stepping down to the bar. Rows of pillars were picked out in primary colours, a seering contrast to the saturated colours of the floor and walls in hot reds, blues and yellows, and Mariscal's etched glass mural behind the bar. There were oval-shaped tables, a large geometric tile mural on one wall, and extensive use of back-lit blue glass for curving walls. The sweeping bar, which shadowed the shape of the gallery above, had a back-lit glass panel decorated with Mariscal's drawings which stretched the entire length of the bar. This panel depicted the various elements of a good party: a table laden with bubbling champagne and glasses, hats being thrown in the air, chairs, and other motifs suggesting conviviality and excitement. Like all good Spanish drinking bars, Duplex

"Lack of Forethought":
a comment on the design
of the Merbeyé bar, 1978.
Fernando Amat asks
Mariscal: "What are
we going to do?"

Fernando Amat, responsible for the interior of the Merbeyé bar, 1978, asked Mariscal to get involved. They took surrealist liberties with the structure, allowing whirling fans to slice through the columns

Altogether more ambitious than Merbeyé was the Duplex bar in Valencia, designed with Fernando Salas in 1980. They made a lot of glass brick and tiled murals in secondary colours and the famous Duplex stool made its first appearance

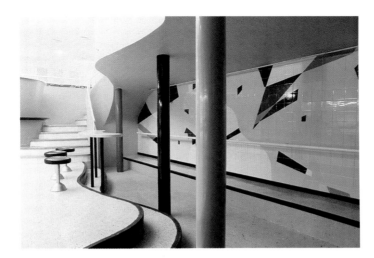

**1950s modernism in the
original drawing for the
Duplex bar poster, 1980**

came alive at night when its long bar filled up and drinkers spilled over the complex interlocking layers, designed to put the people at the bar on show. The main space was sparsely furnished, with just a few tables, cantilevered eccentrically from bullet-shaped pillars.

But the most enduring by-product of this project is the *Duplex* stool, originally designed for the bar, but now in mass production. The stool, five lines held together by what seems like pure chance, looks as if it's about to leap over the bar and head-butt the barman. For many, its shape symbolises everything that is Mariscal. Three legs – one curved grey-blue, one straight red, and one wiggley yellow – are connected by two circular steel braces, one black and one white. A grey-blue, white-piped seat completes the picture. The stool's outlines bring the scratchy energy of Mariscal's drawings to life. "It's unstable. It isn't a stool for fat old men who have to sit there all day in comfort – it's for young people who are nervous, as you are when you want to chat someone up. It's ironic. It's an object that's been in a fight, or on the booze," says Mariscal of his creation. The Barcelona manufacturer and retailer B.D Ediciones de Diseño began to produce the Duplex stool in 1983 – the first piece of Mariscal's furniture to go into production. Its quirky wit and sharp colour sense transformed a low-cost, simply manufactured piece into an instantly recognisable trademark for the new Spanish design. The chair made a quick leap from the pages of Mariscal's sketchbook into three dimensions. The strength of the idea is what gives the chair its power, not the quality of its manufacture or the elegance of its detailing. As such, it is closer to the cartoon quality of the sliced columns and whirling fans of the Merbeyé bar than to conventional mainstream furniture. But then Mariscal had no intention of producing conventional mainstream furniture.

Fernando Amat helped to push Mariscal further down the road to furniture design. In 1981, he asked Mariscal to come up with an exhibition of furniture which was called *Muebles Amorales* [Amoral Furniture]: a none-too-subtle dig at what Mariscal saw as the malign influence of the Bauhaus puritans on contemporary design, with their fetishistic celebration of morality and consistency. As with the Duplex stool, Mariscal's fluent drawing style heavily influences these pieces. The *Gaidó* chair has oddly angled legs – three of them with little waves and one of them straight. The back is an irregular four-sided shape, as is the seat; both are covered in contoured foam rubber. His *Copa Luz* table has the stand and inverted triangle shape of a cocktail glass – the stand black, the base frosted glass, ringed with tubular steel, and a circular glass top; it is illuminated from within. The *Imposible* lamp has a curved and angled upright, leaning forward to support a fluorescent bulb which projects backwards through another bulb which is circular. Mariscal's drawings were turned into prototype pieces of furniture in a string of little back street workshops, capable of manipulating metal, and timber, but without the sophisticated skills or machinery needed to produce more complex designs. His pieces all relied on strong story lines, rather than ingenious technology or detailing.

The exhibition was staged in the Sala Vinçon gallery, a handsome space at the top of Amat's flamboyant nineteenth-century store on the Paseo de Gracia. It was a place which showed serious art and photography as well as furniture, and had already been attracting a lot of attention abroad. An Italian journalist saw the Mariscal exhibition, put the Duplex stool on the cover of *Modo*, and told Ettore Sottsass that it was worth a look. Sottsass, then setting up the Memphis group which, not entirely tongue-in-cheek, he claimed to see as an alternative international style, flew over to see the exhibition for himself, hoping to add a Spanish name to the English, Japanese and Americans that he had already recruited to bolster the Italian contingent. To Mariscal's amazement, Sottsass subsequently asked him to come to Milan. Spanish designers, it should be remembered, were still suffering from an acute inferiority complex. What high design manufacturers there were, relied on overseas talent. So when Mariscal was asked to come up with a design for Memphis, for which he duly produced a number of sketches, the Spanish design community was both impressed, and piqued, at the recognition that this outsider had attracted.

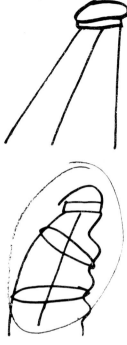

Two sketches for the
Duplex stool (above),
and the final product
(right), produced by B.D
since 1983. The legs play
visual games with logic.
Mariscal calls it "a chair
for the restless"

Three prototypes for the exhibition *Muebles Amorales* at Sala Vinçon, 1981: the Gaidó chair (above), the Copa Luz table (below) and the Imposible lamp (right)

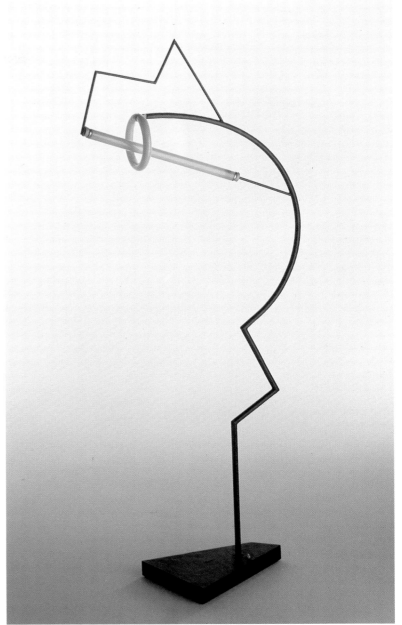

Designed in collaboration with Pepe Cortés, 1981, the Hilton trolly (opposite), was produced by Memphis, Milan, and marked Mariscal's international début

At this point, Mariscal called on his friend Pepe Cortés, who, as an industrial designer, could provide the technical ability which Mariscal lacked to turn the drawings into viable pieces of furniture. This was the first of many Cortés/Mariscal collaborations; the former's technical mind and the latter's wild imagination complemented each other perfectly. It was also a major step for Mariscal, moving him on from what was still seen as a provincial outpost into the sophisticated Milanese scene.

Mariscal's *Hilton* trolley was featured as part of the first Memphis collection in the stifling heat of the Milan Furniture Fair in September 1981. Intended as a drinks trolley, its backwards slant suggests movement, while the three pairs of wheels and sturdy supports suggest strength. There are dashes of colour on the handle and the front "bumper" of this unaffectedly playful piece. Mariscal was asked to produce more designs for Memphis, notably a stool. It never saw the light of day, and Mariscal will still not be drawn on what happened, saying only: "Sottsass likes things to be done his way. Although I always got on with him very well personally, I was never regarded as a designer as I couldn't draw plans; I was an outsider." His disappointment at not being asked to design for Memphis again is obvious. Mariscal still has a number of drawings for other projects for Memphis which never materialised.

Meanwhile, Mariscal was experimenting with surface pattern and working of ceramics. Pep Molins, a friend from Gran Hotel days, worked with him on various objects and sculptures. Together they created the shapes, then Mariscal painted them by hand. Plates, a teapot, and cups and saucers were decorated with his *Abstractos* design – yellow and green washes bisected by black lines and dots – fifties again, but a very subtle evocation rather than an elaborate reproduction. Although working in areas which were financially unrewarding at the time, Mariscal was taking himself closer to the point where he could look for commissions for this type of work.

Another visitor to the Muebles Amorales exhibition had been the

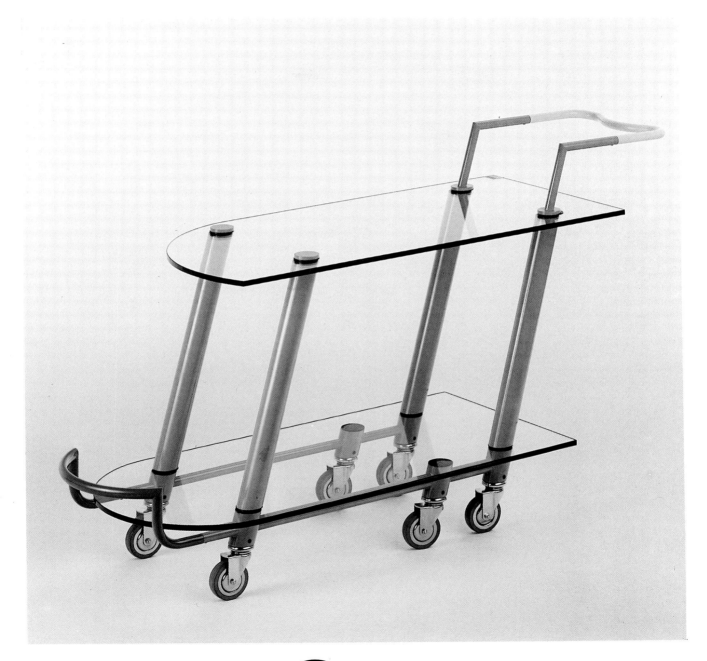

Ceramics decorated in
the Abstractos design –
prototypes by Eduardo
Pastor (1981)

Hand-painted plate (top) and bowl (above) in the Kandinsky range, produced by Vinçon and manufactured by J. Aguadé in 1985

Barcelona textiles company Marieta, which had already used Mariscal to produce a few designs for them after Gran Hotel. A major commission for textile designs marked the beginning of a long-term relationship which eventually encompassed carpets, towels and rugs. One of his earliest designs for them was Kabul, which had rows of squares with Islamic arches, lettering and symbols in rich colours. In it, are found views of everyday life such as a modern kitchen overlooking an Eastern cityscape, busy city-streets, and symbols of the modern world such as streetlamps, cars, trucks and robots. From a distance it looks very Eastern and evocative of the Islamic world; only close-up do you see what the motifs really are. Elements of this design were used on a plastic-coated carrier bag. Other prints included a batik-like fish motif, and there were a number of cotton Jacquards which were first produced in 1983.

As his work became better known, Mariscal found himself increasingly in demand. His next exhibition, staged by B.D, signalled an explosion of new work for Mariscal which coincided with the rise of the design world in Barcelona. B.D Ediciones de Diseño asked Mariscal to produce an exhibition for their gallery in the architecturally spectacular B.D shop in Barcelona in 1983. Mariscal had already worked with Pepe Cortés, and once more he was asked to collaborate on this show. "Pepe helped me to understand what design is. I really needed someone like him to be able to work," Mariscal says.

Mariscal and Cortés produced a show with a broad scope, showing not only furniture and lighting, but rugs as well. This exhibition, *Muebles muy Formales* [Very Formal Furniture], was an obvious progression from the Vinçon show, with similar visual language. The most lasting images from this show were the *Araña* [Spider] lamp, low and floor-standing with three spidery zigzagged legs supporting an inverted disc body which held the light; the *Valencia* lamp, with a forward-leaning upright holding various geometric shapes; and the *Kabul, Sensible* and *Klee-Next* rugs. The Kabul was an interpretation of his Marieta textile design, where Kabul meets cartoon-land, while the

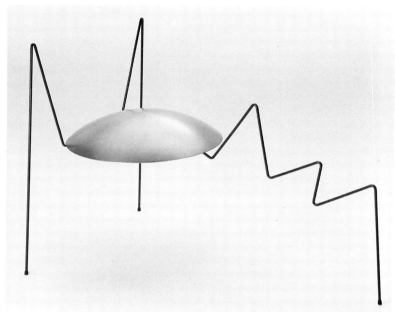

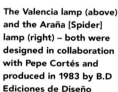

The Valencia lamp (above) and the Araña [Spider] lamp (right) – both were designed in collaboration with Pepe Cortés and produced in 1983 by B.D Ediciones de Diseño

Sensible was composed of abstract patterns, in earthy colours inspired by the East. Some of these designs were put into production by B.D.

Clearly, Cortés was responsible for encouraging Mariscal's move toward mainstream design – as was the venue. B.D was a firm that had combined reproduced Gaudí designs with new pieces by such entirely serious architects as Alvaro Siza and Oscar Tusquets. Mariscal's work as a furniture designer has been much criticised by part of the more established design world in Spain, but he has always seen his own limitations: "I don't make furniture – I make images. My furniture is often philosophical, expressing a way of thinking or provoking a reaction. I do not produce solutions, or try to supply a part of the market like most designers, I am more interested in the decorative aspect." Certainly Mariscal has the knack of creating arresting pieces which, while they appear more two-dimensional than furniture designers feel comfortable with, do have power and impact.

Five of the Mariscal siblings, including the only sister, had set up a fashion company in Valencia, called *Tráfico de Modas*, with its own shop. Inevitably, brother Javier was asked to produce some textile designs. Many of his designs are reworkings of his ideas in other media. In 1984, he was asked to work in another fashion area when the shoe company Camper asked him to create surface patterns for leather shoes. He decided on a design using simple brush-strokes, relying on rich colours to tell the story in such a small canvas.

The following year, 1985, saw the realisation of many projects he had been working on for some time, and a Barcelona company, J. Aguadé, began to produce some of his ceramics for Vinçon. One design, which he called *Kandinsky*, was closely related to work he had done with Eduardo Pastor in 1981. More textiles for Marieta came to fruition, including one which is a play on William Morris's Blackbird print. Another print for Tráfico de Modas was a wild representation of bull-fighting, with cartoon bulls, toreros and bull-ring scenes in splashes of red, blue and yellow. It was called *Souvenir*, an ironic view of the icons of tourist Spain, a partial exorcism perhaps of underdevelopment and the "turista" mentality.

Valencia has an impressive modern furniture shop, Luís Adelantado, stretching over five floors of a Modernista building from the 1930s. Like the Barcelona design shops, it has a large gallery space where Mariscal's paintings and drawings are often exhibited. In 1985, Mariscal held a furniture exhibition there. The best known piece for this show was the *Adelantado* sofa, a monolithic piece with an organically shaped back, a simple ovoid seat in contrasting colours (pink and green was one combination) and an arm/table shaped like a bird-table on one end.

The Fundación de Gremios [Trades Union Foundation] commissioned Mariscal to design a huge rug as a wall-hanging for their headquarters in Madrid. The *Cacería Persa* [Persian Hunting Scene] which he created for them in 1986 was an important landmark in Mariscal's career. This project proved that, for all the cartoon-like illustrations, the wacky patterns, the obscure and challenging furniture

Prototype for the Adelantado sofa, (opposite) 1985; the Kabul rug (below), 1983; detail from the Cacería Persa rug (right), 1986

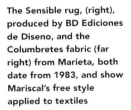

The Sensible rug, (right), produced by BD Ediciones de Diseno, and the Columbretes fabric (far right) from Marieta, both date from 1983, and show Mariscal's free style applied to textiles

Two wall tiles for Neri of Valencia, 1986 (top and centre); and a floor tile for Pamesa, Almazora (above), 1989

that he had been producing for years – much of which was not to everyone's taste – the man was indeed what he always insisted he was: an artist. The Carcería Persa is a masterpiece of drawing, of movement, of colour and of composition. It is a riot of colour and movement, depicting Persian huntsmen on horseback equipped with bows and arrows, chasing leopards, lions, antelope and tigers. It is a mature piece of work, showing Mariscal at his best, and he eventually showed it at the Pompidou Centre in Paris the following year.

The ceramic tile company, Neri of Valencia, commissioned Mariscal for some tile designs. Mariscal was delighted to work in this area: "There are industries in Spain with a great tradition in decorative work. They are good to work for and have great diffusion, so you end up in more people's homes. Now unfortunately, this tradition is being replaced by things that are stupid, ugly and in bad taste." This first commission from Neri led to yet another fruitful relationship: a Parisian ceramic company, Axis, commissioned a series of designs for plates. Mariscal was still designing textiles for Tráfico de Modas, this time a 1986 neo-hippie pattern which was printed by what was arguably Spain's best textile company – Nicky Bosch.

There were two major events for Mariscal in 1986. One was the beginning of a collaboration with the Basque furniture company Akaba. With Pepe Cortés, he designed a sofa, the *M.O.R. Sillón*, which was a visual pun, because the back, a black suede roll held by metal uprights, suddenly takes a right angle and bisects the black-and-white patterned seat. The *Trampolín* chair was another polemical piece, using three materials, three textures and three colours. The base was circular and in grey metal, as was the single leg. The seat was softly curving natural wood, projecting out at the back with a split in it for the back support, a springy metal rod which held the deep-pink upholstered back cushion; when you sit in it the back moves with you. The Trampolín Chair won a prestigious ADIFAD (Agrupación de Disseny Industrial del Foment de les Arts Decoratives) award that year.

When invited to exhibit in the *Nouvelles Tendences* exhibiton held

The M.O.R. Sillón sofa, designed in collaboration with Pepe Cortés in 1986. The name is a pun on the hefty Spanish sausage, the Morcillón, to which the shape of the back cushion bears a more than passing resemblance

as part of the tenth anniversary celebrations of the Pompidou Centre, Mariscal says that he felt ambivalent about the purpose of the show. "It's just the sort of thing that this monster the Pompidou puts together. We were asked to propose our view of the future. Everyone produced *maravillas o tonterías* [wonders or nonsense]. The best thing about it for me was to be able to work for a few days with Philippe Starck, Mendini, Paolo Deganello and Ron Arad." The Pompidou's curators were looking for an encyclopaedic survey of new directions in design, from Future Systems' turbo-charged version of high-tech, to Starck's

Protoypes for two chairs produced by Akaba, Lasarte (Guipúzcoa) in 1987. The Garriri (top) was based on Piker, while the Torera (above) played a game of double bluff with the kitsch view of tourist Spain

seductive neo-deco. They wanted co-operation between participants; instead they got an incoherent series of side-shows. Mariscal's contribution was one of the most straightforward.

Mariscal's recent work with Akaba prompted the suggestion that the company should sponsor and manufacture his work for the show. Mariscal's four chairs for the exhibition were perhaps the most extreme examples of his use of graphic symbols in furniture. All of the pieces played on icons of Spanish life. The *Tío Pepe* chair took the Tío Pepe sherry symbol – the man in the Spanish riding hat with a handlebar moustache – and used this for the back of an almost entirely two-dimensional chair, with no upholstery and straight black legs. The *Garriri* chair took the shape of Mariscal's cartoon-character mouse in chrome, leather and aluminium, to create a dinky little chair with big black ears and clumpy feet. The *Torera* chair had an uncompromisingly improbable metal grid seat, and a black astrakan back in the shape of a bullfighter's hat. The last chair, the *Biscuter*, borrowed its shape from a scooter, rather low and dumpy, with a wheel at the front and with a back borrowed from the Trampolín. It was as if, after flirting with the idea of conventional useable mainstream furniture at the B.D exhibition, Mariscal was now going back to what he felt most comfortable with.

Mariscal was increasingly blurring the distinction between two- and three-dimensional work: his chairs looked like cartoons; his cartoon characters were acquiring more substance. Together with Fernando Amat, Mariscal turned Julián, the dog from his Garriri strip into an object. *Julián, el Perro que Aguanta de Todo* was cast in aluminium. It was definitely a "concept", says Mariscal: "I like to create new functions. For example, Julián is a sculpture which is sold in a little box, and among other functions is that of creating a poetic corner in the home." The Spanish "aguanta" means "bear", so one possible translation would be "the dog who can bear anything", but it can also mean "hold" or "support". Julián is 17-cm high and comes in a box with cartoons explaining how it can be used: "Aguanto libros" [I can support books], and "Aguanto puertas" [I hold open doors]. Julián, the

Two more of Mariscal's cartoon-like furniture creations: the Biscuter (left) and the Tío Pepe chair (above), based on a scooter and the Tío Pepe sherry silhouette repectively, were also produced in 1987 by Akaba, Lasarte (Guipúzcoa)

An aluminium Julián, one of Los Garriris, produced by Vinçon since 1986

Mariscal's neo-classical doorway for the Banco Hispano 20, 1987

perfect pet, is another piece in the jigsaw of Mariscal's work because its realisation, many believe, prompted the Olympic jury to choose Mariscal to design the Olympic mascot.

Mariscal's increasingly high profile was beginning to attract some unlikely establishment clients – even from outside his Barcelona base. The Banco Hispano in Madrid was looking for a new image for the headquarters of Hispano 20, a bank aimed specifically at young people. Mariscal, asked to design a doorway, produced a neo-classical pediment surmounted by typical Mariscal fighting cocks and supported by Ionic and Corinthian columns. The pediment and entablature have friezes depicting the Mariscal view of banks. In the centre is the tree that money *does* grow on, with a magnificent cityscape to one side, and an aeroplane setting down on a palm-strewn island on the other. Beneath it, flanked by a pair of rampant barking dogs, a bank robbery is taking place, with a masked and armed raider facing a terrified policeman. Elegant neo-classicism is subverted by Mariscal's amiable disrespect for authority.

Collaborations with Tráfico de Modas continued, as well as with Marieta, for whom he designed a range of monochrome patterns. Textile and rug manufacturer Nani Marquina, well known for inviting top designers from around the world to design limited edition pieces, also commissioned Mariscal, who gave them the *Estambul* rug design, another reworking of a Turkish design.

Nineteen eighty-eight was also a good year for Mariscal. He finally gained international credibility and prestige for perhaps the least understood area of his work when his cartoon character Cobi was selected as the official Olympic mascot for the 1992 games in Barcelona. In the lead-up to the competition and since, Mariscal's pace has not slowed down. Jewelery in the form of metal, gold and silver pins, brooches and earrings of his cartoon characters were produced for the Barcelona company Cha-Cha. A lush scarlet rose pattern was produced for Tráfico de Modas. His wonderful *León Solitario* rug, with a grinning lion standing in splendid isolation in the middle of a deep

Bedlinen produced by Burés, 1988. "Muy Buenas Noches" [A Very Good Night] is scrawled on the bottom sheet, "Buenos Días"on the turnover

Piker Dando Vueltas al Mundo, part of a range of ceramics designed for Bidasoa in 1988

blue expanse, was produced for Nani Marquina. The linen manufacturer Burés, who had previously employed the likes of fashion designer Sybilla, commissioned sets of bedsheets. One had *Muy Buenas Noches* [A Very Good Night] printed in black on the bottom sheet, and *Buenos Días* [Good Morning] embroidered in yellow on the turnover; others had typical light Mariscal border patterns, or all-over prints in rich colours.

Mariscal also produced his first work for the ceramics company Bidasoa in 1988. This was particularly important for him because of his view of "culture" in everyday life: "I imagine a table with four plain white plates, and some very correct cups, so you need a touch of something else. It could be a salt-cellar or a bowl or a dish, but something light and happy, not strictly necessary," he explains, referring to the decorative table ceramics, some chicken sculptures and flower vases which he has designed. He also designed motifs for hand-painting on to existing shapes such as tea-sets, plates and bowls. Some drew on his repertoire of cartoon characters – *Piker dando Vueltas al Mundo* [Piker running around the World], *Paisaje Metafísico* [Metaphysical Landscape], with Piker in strange abstract surroundings, and a Mariscal version of Milton Glazer's "I ♥ NY", with skyscrapers and lines of cars. One set of six plain white plates had black painted and inscribed borders, with line-drawn pictures of strange birds perching on even stranger trees.

"This work is food for the mind of the people. We need to eat every day to survive, and in the same way I believe that we need culture – we need to eat culture every day. I deal in the culture of the image which creates a daily dialogue with society", he says.

For his architectural projects, Mariscal depended on his relationship with a series of collaborators, the most important of which has turned out to be the Barcelona architect Alfredo Arribas. The spectacular *Gambrinus Restaurant* on the Moll de la Fusta is part of a refurbishment scheme for the docks of Barcelona, a long-neglected district which was being remodelled as a new recreation area. The

Two cubist flower vases
in the porcelain collection
produced by Bidasoa,
Irún, Guipúzcoa

Porcelain plates and a centre-piece (below, left) for Bidasoa. All feature designs with stylised trees and animals and were first produced in 1988

The architect Alfredo Arribas, who frequently collaborates with Mariscal

Arribas and Mariscal's Interior for Clik dels Nens (below), a children's room at the Museu de la Ciència, and Mariscal's poster for the installation (bottom), summer 1989

overall scheme had rerouted a busy traffic artery in order to create a wide promenade where four restaurant bars had been built to similar design; the design of the interiors was handed over to the emerging stars of Spain's design profession. Arribas, who won the commission in the first place, brought in Mariscal to add spice to his architectural approach. Arribas designed a wooden boat-shaped bar and galley for cooking, complete with portholes. The dining area has the flavour of a 1920s ocean liner; comparatively restrained, and lit with oblique-angled lamps. Mariscal was mainly responsible for the exterior terrace, for which he designed a Robinson Crusoe-like shipwreck scene. Tables and benches are made of "driftwood", and are shaded by parasols also made from "driftwood" and tattered pieces of fabric, apparently lashed together by shipwrecked sailors mixing metal and wood. The level of detail is ingenious and subtle: legs have wheels on them; some of the metal chairs have octopus or fish shapes. But what the building has become known for around the world is Mariscal's outrageous roof-top lobster – diners are greeted by a 15-metre-high grinning crustacean.

The success of this first collaboration with Arribas was followed by two other interior projects. *El Clik dels Nens* [loosely translated as "Kids' Thing"] is a pioneering project in Barcelona's Science Museum. Like many modern museums, Barcelona wanted to popularise science for children, by creating a interactive space that brought basic principles to life in an attention-grabbing way. The result is Mariscal's favourite project. "El Clik" is on the ground floor in a long windowed gallery. It is entered through a number of doorways along a corridor just off the main reception area. The various installations change periodically, but it is worth visualising how it was in summer 1989: on entering the corridor, you are confronted by a solid, rock-like ramp which, when you scale it, turns out to be rubber. There is a patch of doormatting, and a series of marble piano keyboard steps – walking down, each step plays a different note. This is an observation lesson in textures. Along the corridor are interactive videos programmed with

The world-famous cheeky lobster of Gambrinus seafood restaurant on El Moll de la Fusta, a combined effort by Arribas and Mariscal, 1988. The lobster was made by Monolo Martín

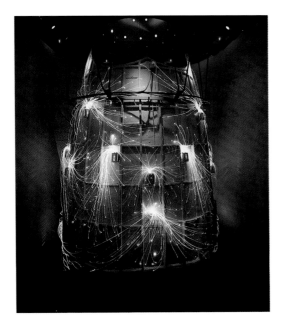

Completed in 1990, the nightclub Las Torres de Ávila (opposite and above) was carved from a 1920s replica of a medieval gateway, and was Mariscal and Arribas's largest and most complex project to date, mixing metaphysics with theatre

simple games. The doorways into the main gallery are child-sized, and are entered via ramps. Inside are a number of installations conceived by the museum staff and designed by Arribas and Mariscal. There are telephones which make animal noises, semi-reflective screens where you compare your own height with that of various animals, a giant Newton's cradle and a bubble fountain. In another installation, three identical life-sized hippos are strung from fulcrums of different lengths. By pulling a handle or sitting on a bar, you discover how many children are needed to lift the hippo. Arribas's loos are child-sized, but otherwise they would suit any of his wondrous night-clubs. They have cleverly angled screens rather than doors, with tiny sinks, and specially low windows so that children can look out into the courtyard.

The most dramatic Mariscal/Arribas production is that of *Las Torres de Ávila*, a spectacular interior project for a nightclub which shows what Mariscal is capable of when he goes beyond the cartoon quirkiness of his origins. It has the dramatic gestures of Gambrinus, but instead of being content to play with toy-like juxtapositions of scale, and winsome colour, Torres de Ávila is an ambitious piece of narrative architecture. It is situated in El Pueblo Español, high up in Montjuich Park, where a kitsch collection of full-size reproductions of traditional Spanish houses was built for the 1929 International Exhibition – a kind of nationalist version of Disneyland. Now that the passing of time has safely taken the sting out of the kitschness of the original idea, the Pueblo Español has been restored and a number of upmarket restaurants and bars have moved in, between the tourist shops. The impressive fortified gatehouse for the village is a re-creation of Las Torres de Ávila, the medieval entrance to the town of Ávila. In this extraordinary space, the designers' imaginations ran wild.

The Gothic exterior provided the institutional starting point for the interior, which has been described as "*una neo-mazmorra*" [a neo-dungeon]. Inside, a series of mystical themes combine with disorientating spatial tricks. A circuitous route up a sloping wooden ramp leads to the first-floor entrance, and the first taste of confusion:

Mariscal's graphics from Las Torres de Ávila include murals as well as direction signs and stationery

the doorway looks too low to negotiate. On crossing a downward-curving bridge, however, you discover that there is adequate headroom after all. Seizing on the twin towers of the gateway, the conversion is based on a series of yin/yang opposites. The right-hand tower is intended to represent day and masculinity; the left, embodies the nocturnal and feminine. A perilous metal stairway criss-crosses between the two towers.

The main bar, dark and womb-like, is furnished in honey-coloured suede. The interior walls, inscribed with weird cabalistic symbols and figures, are studded with tiny lights like the night sky; the exterior is swathed in a complex pattern of fibre-optic entrails that recreate the spooky sensation of a high-tech science fiction filmset. On the gallery level, the anxiety-producing impact of the transparent glass floor is heightened by a constantly changing lighting system. One moment, the floor appears solid; the next, it plunges into a vertiginous void – to the audible discomfort of those drinking there. Meanwhile, a TV-screen set into the ceiling relays, with nerve-jangling rapidity, a sequence of images of the human eye. Above, there is an even more extraordinary bar. Set in the arch that links the towers, it has glass walls, a steeply sloping floor carpeted with coir matting, and a glass pyramid roof with a masonic eye inside a triangle at the apex. Two floor-to-ceiling windows open out over an eighty-foot drop.

The spectacular roof terrace overlooking Montjuic Park is divided into two areas. The night side, a black dome which Mariscal decorated with stars, comets and a moon, sits over a circular opening. The day-side dome, crowned by the sun, covers a glass cylinder that drops down the full height of the building. Within this, a suspended globe moves silently up and down, announcing its arrival with flashing lights. Torres de Ávila is typical of the projects that Arribas and Mariscal have worked on together and their presence is felt at every level. Throughout the club, the choice of materials and the finish achieved is remarkable. Nevertheless, the overall atmosphere of the club is rather tense. If you do find a quiet corner, it will be overlooked by a headless

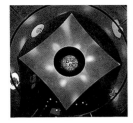

Interior views of Las Torres de Ávila, showing the descending canopy (top and right) and a headless winged creature (above). (Overleaf) the sun and moon towers of the roof terrace at night

Mariscal's mural in one of the link bars (opposite) between the two Ávila towers. (Overleaf) Mariscal's screen for Alfredo Arribas's Barna Crossing project

winged creature, a gargole, or some other phantasma. "There is a lot of play in this project", Mariscal understates, "it stretches the concept of a bar – you either love it or hate it."

As with all of his collaborations, the division of who does what is hard to define. Mariscal says: "Arribas is obsessed by perfection. He is the truck, I am the trailer, but we share decisions about the structure – where there should be a window or a hole, how you enter, the whole concept and philosophy of the project. Las Torres is very intellectual, and could provoke new sensations; it is like the end of ideologies."

Having created the club-to-end-all-clubs, it is hard to imagine where the Mariscal/Arribas team can go from here. Perhaps Las Torres will be seen in retrospect as the high-point of the wave of Barcelona bars of the 1980s, though it did follow hard on the heels of the Barna Crossing project in the Japanese city of Fukuoka. Here, Arribas, who was designing the basement bar in a hotel designed by Aldo Rossi, asked Mariscal to provide oil paintings, murals and fixtures. And the Mariscal-Arribas team showed no sign of running out of ideas, even though the pressure of the fashion system on design was pushing them to come up with ever more spectacular interiors. Mariscal is certainly very much aware of changing moods and attitudes in the 1990s. It has been some years since he designed a piece of furniture, a conscious decision on his part: "To make really interesting furniture, I need a little leisure and relaxation – a little more maturity. I would like to bring out something very new, with more weight and more interest. It was fine in the eighties, but I think that the epoch of making amusing furniture has passed."

Chapter Four

**Julián en el Atlántico,
acrylic on coloured
drawing paper, 1984**

While some critics would claim that Mariscal is a large talent in a minor art, he himself has no such qualms. "There is no art with a capital 'A' or art with a little 'a'," says Mariscal. "I see comic strips as having the same value as a painting. I feel the same emotional charge looking at a painting by Matisse as I do with some comics. For me there is no difference between enjoying a painting by Goya, a good television programme, a good advert, a theatrical work, riding a roller-coaster, or reading a comic book." Mariscal claims he first discovered the great masters in the picture cards that came with a particular brand of chocolates in his childhood. The anarchy of Pop Art, and its celebration of the mundane, appealed to him strongly: "Without Pop Art, I would not exist", he says, "Pop shows you how to evaluate other medias, some already in existence, others that are still emerging."

Mariscal makes no distinction between the different types of work he does. Nor does he think that his role, as what most people would call a "designer", is qualitatively different from the role of his friends from the early days who are still working on comic strips. He likes to be working on lots of different things at the same time, and might be working on a logo one day, a chair the next, a painting the next. All are done in the same studio and are treated as work: "Mi trabajo es un proyecto de arte," he says [All my work is a project of art], adding as an ironic aside that he calls it "art" because then it sells better. He also asserts: "The only thing I do better than draw is sell. I'm a great salesman. I do it all by phone. My objects are on the margin – somewhere between the shop and the gallery." All this candour is a long way from the overblown claims made about the questionable work of the New York graffiti school, which has in some ways been regarded as comparable with that of Mariscal. Yet Mariscal certainly does have a very painterly preoccupation with light. "It seems to me that even mid-day sun – the most objective kind of light – in fact makes things look completely unreal. My work is based on what you see in the street, those glances at posters, shop windows, bars, cars, chairs, the light from a street-lamp, the roof of a shack," he explains.

Mariscal's view of Gaudí's Barcelona: The Sagrada Familia (right), drawing, 1987 and La Pedrera [The Quarry] (below), drawing, 1987. Other local heroes receive more sardonic treatment: León Azul [Blue Lion] (far right, top), painting, 1989; Juanito Miró saluda a Pepa Pizza con su Paraguas en una Tórrida Tarde de Arena [Johnny Miró greets Pepa Pizza with his Brolly on a Torrid, Dusty Afternoon] (far right, middle), glass painting, 1990

Gato Sonriente [Smiling Cat] (right), drawing, 1988 and Garriris en Cala Marsal [Garriris in Marsal Cove] (far right), painting, 1986

There was a time in the mid-seventies when he wanted to be a "real" painter. He was close to Miguel Barceló, now a well-known painter, and desperately wanted to emulate him, working in oil on canvas, with little success. Mariscal then decided to try a medium he had always admired, the traditional art of glass painting – in some ways a more natural progression from the comics he was doing at the time.

Glass painting is not a simple process. Initial pencil sketches are transferred on to tracing paper. This is placed picture-side down with the glass on top of it and the outlines are then copied on to this. When this has dried, the other block colours are added. As you work from the back of the glass, the picture is seen the other way round; in other words, you cannot paint over mistakes. Seen through glass, the colours have great intensity, and this gives the paintings their special quality.

Mariscal produced many such glass paintings for his first two exhibitions: *Gran Hotel* in 1977, and *Decorapart* the following year, which was shown in Fernando Amat's gallery Detrás-Vinçon [literally, "behind Vinçon], the precursor of the Sala Vinçon gallery . They reworked 1950s themes – travel by ocean liner, cocktails, glamour – and borrowed heavily from the advertisements for various dishes seen in the cafés of his youth. At the time he was working as *Gráficos y Vidrios Mariscal* with Félix Preciado and his brothers Pedrín and Santi Errando. Marieta used one of his pictures of salad as a print on a tray.

His first major exhibition of exclusively two-dimensional work was held at the Galería Central in Madrid. There were paintings in a variety of media, pastels, and a number of glass paintings. Also included was a tribute to Hockney's Splash paintings, several energetic night-time traffic scenes and a sentimental look at *Julia Swimming*, showing a patch of sand with his daughter's recently vacated shoes and a bucket and spade.

In a very different mode, the Galería Temple in Valencia showed some of his line drawings, executed during a visit to Japan. The simple black-on-white, angular, laughing Japanese in his pictures are a stark contrast to the vivid, luscious and eccentric drawings inspired by

Barcelona. His visit to Tokyo presented him with the opportunity to emulate one of his great heroes, Kandinsky. The story, as told by Fernando Amat, who accompanied him, is that they were spending an evening with a Japanese business man, who happened to be a brother of the owner of a big local hotel. He told them that, many years ago, Kandinsky had stayed in the hotel, and spent many hours over his breakfast table, mixing colours and trying them out on the china in front of him. Rather than objecting, the man had the foresight to put the china to one side and keep it. He had the painted china displayed in a cupboard in his office. The Kandinsky-loving Mariscal and Amat insisted on seeing the pieces, but Satomi explained that he and his brother had argued some years before and were not on speaking terms. He would obviously have to be induced.

One of a series of drawings from Mariscal's trip to Japan in 1983

健康優良児た

エクササイズ・パーティ

Paintings on glass:
Compañía Transatlántica
(above), 1978; and Platos
Combinados, (right), 1978

Las Meninas (above,
after Velázquez) 1990
and Les Carotes
(Almazora) (left) 1980

Pollo Chuleta sculpture for the exhibition Esculturas Adelantadas en el Nuevo Estilo Post-Barroco: polyurethane painted to resemble bronze, 1986

After trying, unsuccessfully, to drink Satomi under the table, they all went out to eat. Faced for the first time with chopsticks and tofu, the two Spaniards proceeded to make complete fools of themselves and Satomi began to laugh helplessly. Inspiration struck Mariscal: sticking one chopstick through his shaggy locks, and holding the other in his painting hand, he took the bottle of soy sauce and began to draw on a tablecloth. Slowly but surely, every free piece of white linen in the restaurant was turned into a Mariscal landscape of Barcelona, with beaches, streets, bars, Montjuic park and the sea. The clientele watched in speechless wonder. The masterpiece was saved till last, wherein their own table cloth was turned into a Mariscalesque representation of the Sagrada Familia church in mixed media of tofu and various other sauces. Working with lightening speed from top right to bottom left ("a la japonesa"), Mariscal changed the motto carved in stone around the towers to "Gaudí loves Satomi".

They got their way, and Satomi managed to smuggle them into his brother's office in the small hours of the morning. Too cautious to turn on the lights, Satomi used his cigarette lighter to provide light, badly burning his thumbs in the process. Some time later, back in Barcelona, Mariscal suggested using the Kandinsky pattern to brighten up Vinçon's china. He remembered the pattern perfectly.

The next major exhibition after the Galería Temple was at Sala Vinçon in 1986. It was Mariscal's first major venture into sculpture, and went a long way towards overcoming the art world's resistance to his work. Called *Esculturas Adelantadas en el Estilo Post-Barroco* [Advanced Sculptures in the New Post-Baroque Style], the Cubist-inspired pieces were in polyurethane, lacquered to look like bronze. There were still-lifes, chickens, a lion, vases complete with flowers, a clock, and a throne. The most striking piece was the *Chaise-longue Barroca*, an extraordinary chair with anthropomorphic arms, legs and back. It was this exhibition that prompted Juli Capella and Quim Larrea, then editors of *De Diseño*, to devote an entire issue of their magazine to Mariscal.

From the exhibition
Cosquillas para tus Ojos,
Sala Vinçon, 1989:
Ordenador Primera
Generación – conjunto
[First Generation
Computer – suite]; Moto
Ángel Nieto – 20 veces
Campeón del Mundo
[Ángel Nieto, Moped – 20
times World Champion]

That same year, a major Madrid art gallery showed his work during Arco, the annual art fair. The Galería Moriarty had been a pioneering supporter of the Spanish avant-garde La Movida artists, eventually gaining credibility for the movement. The notoriety which followed the adoption of his Cobi as the Olympic mascot attracted even more interest. In 1989 Mariscal was involved in no less than five exhibitions showing: his paintings at Arco with Moriarty again; paintings at the Galería Berini in Barcelona; etchings at the Galería Eude in Barcelona; a new series of sculptures, *Cosquillas para tus Ojos* [Tickles for your Eyes] in Sala Vinçon; and further paintings at the Galería Trayecto in Vitoria.

However, despite all this exposure, Mariscal has been heavily criticised for showing "illustration" in "art" galleries. His bravado belies the fact that the criticism still rankles. He remarks, pointedly, "No one doubts today that Toulouse Lautrec is as important as any of the Post-Impressionists."

Mariscal exhibited a series of watercolours on rice-paper at the Galería Trayecto, Vitoria in 1989 and at Valencia's Luís Adelantado Gallery in 1990. Later that year, he created a new series of glass paintings for exhibitions at the Galería Moriarty, Madrid, and the Galería Berini, Barcelona. "I have been playing with the work of great painters such as Miró and Velázquez. I have stolen them and made them my own," he says. Asked if he sees this as another phase, he retorts: "Look, it's just a joke. I really don't think it's important. It's just another resource."

Another inspiration is travel: "I am always fascinated by absolutely everything, from seeing the place where mankind was born, to twenty bonsais, or a woman pouring out a bottle of water. I have a great curiosity and want to have a look in at every corner of the world." But wherever he goes he is always drawn to the sea, which is a constant presence in much of his work. "The sea is always there, like a mirror of the sky; it can be blue, marine, green, emerald, grey, brown, black, darker than the sky, lighter than the sky, silver grey like a dead thing, or a rich algae green, rather dirty. Or, it can be a blue which gives you

Posters for the Santa Cruz
de Tenerife carnival (top),
for the *Festa de la Lletra*
group exhibition (above),
and for the Correfoc
event of Barcelona's
Mercè '83 festival (right)

Amanita Circus poster produced for the theatre group La Claca, 1986

Glass painting of "Spain, the New Rising Star", 1990 – the design was too much for Bloomingdale's sensibilities

incredible happiness in the morning when you see it, with a variety of colours like a Hockney swimming pool."

Many critics have commented on the Cubist element in his work, and he attributes this to the light in Spain. Speaking again about the midday sun, what he considers to be the most realistic light, he explains: "the façade of a house could be black or white – the shadows completely destroy the architecture, making it look unreal, but you could say that this is the 'Real Time'. With such brutal light everything is chopped off as if with an axe. In England, the light is more filtered and soft – you can't really see the outline of a house or a tree, and when the sun goes down you have three hours of melancholy. You can't have Cubism in that light. In Spain when the sun goes to bed, it goes running."

The parts of the world he doesn't like are Florence ("It's like a museum or a cemetery, you can't step on anything"), New Zealand ("They park neatly, inside yellow lines"), and San Francisco ("so false, like a wedding cake"). The places he likes particularly are Benidorm ("totally chaotic, so extreme it's enchanting"), Los Angeles ("A city I could have designed"), New York ("I feel at home – such a mixture of races – like a big sandwich"), and Barajas Airport in Madrid ("It's anti-design, you can see the very human incapacity to organise, I see it as very beautiful").

Many of his trips, of course, are for work. Bloomingdale's in New York have involved Mariscal in both of their Spanish promotions, one in 1987 and the other in 1990. For the second of these he was again asked to produce an illustration for posters and carrier bags. For the previous one, he had drawn a totally innocuous woman's face, with a very Spanish kiss-curl. This time he wanted to go a little further. His new design, Spain, the New Rising Star, featured a statuesque female figure being mounted by a bull – for him, the essence of Spain. Bloomingdale's were shocked, and faxed back a suggestion that he put the woman in a bra, move the bull to one side, and slice the whole illustration through the middle. Mariscal would not have his picture

**Local landmarks inspired
The Abecedari Barcelona
alphabet, created in 1986**

**Mariscal's cover for
Fuego en las Entrañas, by
Pedro Aldomóvar, 1981**

tampered with, and sent back his fee, commenting: "Poor things, we are going forwards and they are going backwards."

Many of Mariscal's commissioned illustrations, for organisations inside or outside the city, feature Barcelona in one of its many manifestations. Mariscal never tires of his adopted city and reworks it constantly. He has produced so many logos, illustrations and graphics for Spain's most fashionable bars, restaurants and shops, that it would be literally impossible to catalogue them all. There have been record covers, badges and posters, in later years more and more for established organisations such as banks, and for the city council promoting trade shows and festivals.

In 1978, Mariscal's first typeface, *ABCDari Il.lustrat*, was featured in the series Quaderns Crema, produced by the Barcelona publisher A. Bosch, Editores, under the direction of Jaume Vallcorba Plana. The following year, his famous *Bar Cel Ona* [Bar/Sky/Wave] picture was adopted for a promotional poster for the city. It has since been reproduced endlessly, most notably on a T-shirt in 1984 and a poster in 1986. Another play on the name "Barcelona" was produced, but never used, for the Mercè '86 festival, organised by the Ajuntament de Barcelona. Mariscal used architectural features and icons of the city to make up the letters for his *Abecedario Barcelona* [Barcelona Alphabet]. It was later developed for the exhibition *Cent Anys a Barcelona*, and was eventually applied to pins, T-shirts, towels and souvenirs produced by Cha-Cha.

Mariscal put together the cover and a number of black-and-white illustrations for Pedro Almodóvar's book, *Fuego en las Entrañas* , printed in 1981. He has also produced material for a several magazines, including covers for *Ambassador,* TWA's in-flight magazine and *La Luna de Madrid,* the magazine connected with La Movida.

Recurrent themes in Mariscal's pictures include children, especially babies and toddlers, dogs, girls in mini-skirts out on the town, boys on the make, robbers (who conveniently always wear masks and striped clothes for easy identification), VW mini-buses blaring music, heavy

In his graphics for
El Tragaluz restaurant,
Mariscal created two new
"typefaces" for the eating
areas, using stylised food
symbols for letters

Mariscal's identity for
the Barcelona jeweller
Colomer uses a number
of recognisable motifs

drinking, parties and clubs, beaches, scooters, various icons of the city of Barcelona, avant-garde furniture and architecture, and seafood.

This last subject was the inspiration behind the restaurant *Gambrinus*, which he designed with Alfredo Arribas in 1988, and for much of the furniture, etched-glass windows, and restaurant logo, which was created in collaboration with Sonsoles Llorens. The massive three-dimensional lobster on the roof was also featured more discreetly in the restaurant's graphics. Another collaboration with Llorens the same year was for the Cromosoma TV production company. Pepe Cortés was responsible for the complete restructuring and interior design of a new restaurant, *El Tragaluz* [The Skylight] in central Barcelona in 1990, where Mariscal's graphics were used on the façade, the menus, napkins, placemats and even woven into the tablecloths.

The Cobi commission allowed Mariscal to move his studio out of his home and into a former tannery. He then made the transition from a one-man cottage industry into an executive, coping with the staff and technology that comes with running a design consultancy with a portfolio of international clients. The transition has not always been easy one, and Mariscal has called in various partners and associates to try to impose some sense of commercial discipline into the creative chaos with which he runs his life.

Mariscal has always had an exhibitionistic streak, and has made videos of all his exhibitions, some rather eccentric, with himself as the commentator. For Gran Hotel he shot a futuristic video, *Vida en Común* [Communal Life], which related to the way he had been living for the past few years. His obsession with keeping and recording everything he has done is a rather mystifying aspect of Mariscal's character, almost as if he sees his life as a comic strip, with every event "framed" for posterity. The video he made for the public visiting the *100 Años con Mariscal* exhibition in Valencia was a piece of obvious showmanship. He didn't want the public to think that, despite the title and purpose of the exhibition, Mariscal takes himself too seriously. He says that he wanted the exhibition to be like a supermarket, with everything there

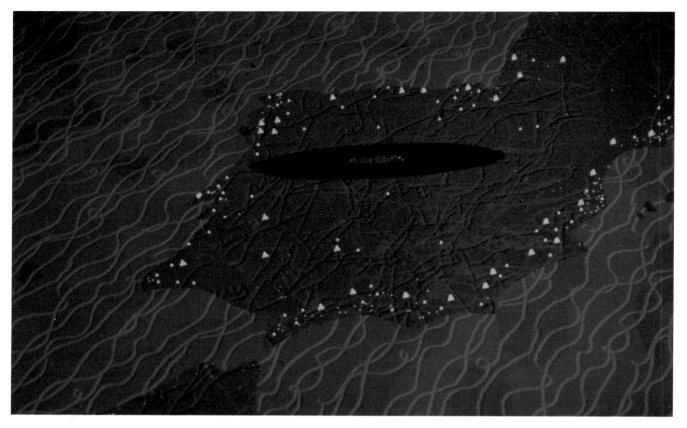

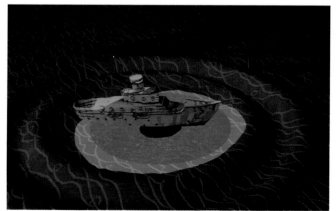

Mariscal's logo for the radio station Onda Cero plays on the ambiguity of symbols for a wave [onda] and zero [cero]. (Opposite) three images from the Onda Cero television campaign, 1990

"accessible and cheap". The video portrays Mariscal in white top hat and tails, singing a song about himself and in his work as he strides, Busby Berkeley-style, down a flight of stairs.

Animation and film have always fascinated Mariscal, and he was delighted when, in 1990, he was asked to create a total corporate identity – his first – together with a TV advertising campaign for a new radio station. This station is called *Onda Cero* [Zero Wave] and the logo plays on the name, using two O's, which can be interpreted in a variety of ways. "With a disc you have two circles, so it could be a hole inside a solid, or a solid inside a hole. I wanted to evoke that duality: What is a solid? What is air? What is inside? What is outside? It could be two records, or two ears, or two people, one talking and one listening. It all works well for radio," explains Mariscal.

There are three 30-second spots for the TV campaign, the first of which plays on the ambiguity of the logo. The second turns the logo into a flying saucer with a shadow, zooming over the earth and beaming down on people in a car, a house, a ship at sea; every time the beam hits an object, the object lights up. The third spot has a typical Mariscal couple in different situations: in the street, in the rain, under the moon; when they kiss, the kiss turns into the logo. His characters and colours are superb, using very intense colours which are rarely seen in animation. However, the most interesting aspect of the campaign is that it is all done in 3-D – the first time that three-dimensional animation has been used on TV in Spain.

The colouring is all done mathematically, with a technician actually converting Mariscal's paintings into mathematical formulas. The shapes are produced by plotting models of the objects and buildings with a scanner. This was accomplished with the computerised animation company Animática, and is seen as a tremendously creative use of 3-D. Nevertheless, Mariscal confesses that he is not entirely happy with the results: "When you are working on something which is really new for you, it's frightening. You don't have any references. Certain people say they are awful – really bad."

Cobi at the Olympics

After a selection process that took on as much political as athletic significance, Barcelona failed in its first serious attempt to host the Olympic Games. In the event, the1936 games went to Berlin instead. Undaunted by its failure to attract the official event to Spain, the city's popular-front government staged its own "People's Games" as a riposte to Hitler. But the red sandstone stadium, built high up on the Montjuic Park as a token of the seriousness of Barcelona's committment to staging the 1936 games, was left to rot. It was never used for the purpose it was intended as long as international ostracism of Franco's regime put paid to any fresh attempts to bring the Olympics to Spain for four decades. It was not surprising then that Barcelona, more perhaps than any other city in the recent history of the Olympics, collectively set its heart on staging the games. The city's successful campaign to secure the 1992 games, which came to a climax between 1985 and 1986, was genuinely popular – going far beyond the self-interested cliques of local politicians and businessmen who stage most Olympics bids.

Barcelona was looking for more than the windfall profits that came from selling the TV rights to the proceedings, the sponsorship deals and property speculation. This was a chance for the city to assert its own identity, both in the Spanish, and the international context. Despite all the horse-trading in smoke-filled rooms, the political bargaining, and the wheeling and dealing that accompanied it, the decision of the International Olympic Committee (IOC) to bring the games to Barcelona was greeted with spontaneous celebrations in the city. News of the IOC's decision, relayed over the radio, brought on an outbreak of hooting car horns, and impromptu parties. It set the seal on the Catalan revival and a democratic Spain, a country at last free from the isolation of the Franco years.

Work had begun on planning the games long before the final decision was made to hold them in Barcelona. From the start, the Olympic Games were seen as a catalyst for a wholesale modernisation. Barcelona's nineteenth-century architects had used the staging of the

1888 World's Fair to release the city from the bounds of its medieval core with a new masterplan. In the same way, in the1980s and 1990s, Barcelona's government drew up plans for a city that would emerge from the Olympics with a new airport, new hotels and offices and, above all, with its ancient link with the Mediterranean re-established. For 100 years the city had been cut off from its coastline by a dense wedge of industrial buildings, warehouses and railways. Barcelona has demolished them all to make way for the Olympic Village. After the games, the rebuilt strip between the sea and the old town will become a new residential area for the city.

Money was poured into the project. From its earliest days, the games were seen as an opportunity to bring the talents of the world's best-known architects and designers to the city. Vittorio Gregotti was commissioned to remodel the old Olympic stadium. Norman Foster got the job of designing a rocket-shaped telecommunications mast, Arata Isozaki designed a new stadium, and Ricardo Bofill remodelled the city's airport. All of this monumental architecture, and the civic restructuring that goes with it, will be the lasting legacy of the games. But in the short term, the abiding image of the games for the millions who actually visit Spain, will be that of Mariscal's official Olympic mascot – Cobi, the cubist cartoon dog.

In the months building up to the games, a blizzard of Cobi ephemera overwhelmed the entire city, from the inflatable plastic Cobi dolls attached by plastic suckers to the rear windscreens of the city's taxis, to the much more expensive cast-aluminium versions of the dog on sale in the upmarket design stores. In one city park there is a coin-in-the-slot automaton version of Cobi, negotiating a swimming pool, pursued by a shark. There are badges, and T-shirts, key rings and stickers, all featuring Cobi's instantly recognisable features.

One of six designers invited to take part in a limited competition judged by the Olympic Committee, Mariscal won the commission in 1988. It was both a controversial and a shrewd choice. Mariscal's well publicised, and less-than-serious outburst against the Catalans and

Waiting for the world to
descend on Barcelona:
the official COOB'92 Cobi
poster, 1990

Mariscal's studio worked flat out creating 3-D prototypes of Cobi engaged in various sports (above and opposite)

their government didn't help. In one sense, Mariscal was a risk because he wasn't interested in producing a conventional design for the mascot. On the other hand, it was precisely because it was so much more sophisticated than any of its predecessors that his symbol has proved to be so memorable – and therefore so much more saleable. The scratchy lines of the humanoid dog Cobi came as a sharp contrast to the endless succession of heavy-handed, kitsch or plain inept mascots adopted by the Olympic movement in recent years. Cobi by contrast is sharply drawn, and anything but saccharine-sweet sentimental. He comes in virtually every medium, from metal and plastic sculptures with an animated cartoon strip to follow. More to the point, though prolific in his output, Mariscal's experience as a graphic designer had been limited to commissions that were heavier in their creative input than in their demand for disciplined implementation skills.

However, Mariscal's involvement with the Olympics has gone much further than the creation of a single symbol. He has created an entire cast of characters for the Olympics signage programme. Each sport, from judo to rifle-shooting, features Cobi, delineated by Mariscal in collaboration with Quod Disseny, the studio of Josep María Trias, who produced Barcelona's version of the Olympic logo. The Olympic press corps are given decals featuring Cobi kitted out as a journalist while, at the Olympic hotels, Cobi will be in evidence in a bellboy uniform. Cobi is successful because he works on two levels. Taken at face value, he has the winsome appeal of a pet dog. Yet at the same time, he is also a subversive.

Mariscal has produced a graphic identity programme of daunting complexity, one that is geared not only towards creating an image for the games, but also to the voracious needs of the marketing industry associated with them. Cobi, and characters based on him, will be in evidence throughout the city and the various Olympic sites.

Although the Barcelona games were floated on a tide of high-minded idealism, they were also supported by a hard-headed marketing campaign which budgeted on making millions of dollars from licensing deals, selling the right to exploit the Cobi symbol to the highest bidder. The result is Mariscal's most visible, most powerful, but also his most risky creation. He has always relied on the freshness, and spontaneity, that comes from a lingering sense of being an outlaw that his drawings convey. His work succeeds because it looks as if it has bypassed the polishing effects of large budgets, and elaborate technical facilities, to communicate in a very direct way. Of course, that is exactly how Mariscal started out, committed and personal, rather than bland and corporate. But his commercial success has somewhat transformed the meaning of his work. While retaining the distinctive trademarks of his style, he has adapted his work to higher production values and operating on a vastly larger scale. In so doing, he has had to face up to the sterilising effect of high production values, looking beyond technique to ideas. It is of course a paradoxical position to be in, one that is a little like the dilemma that faced the grafitti artists taken up by mainstream art galleries or the hot rod car-builder asked to take over a production line at a Ford factory. How much of the original charm of the idea will be lost in the translation to a large budget?

The Corporate Cobi appears in many guises: a journalist, a bellboy, and even, as here, a doctor

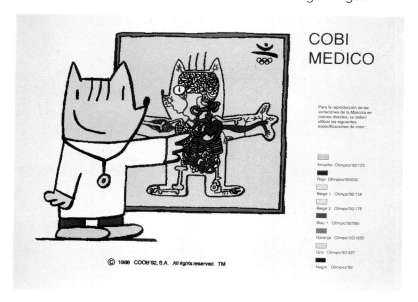

Mariscal remains the court jester, tolerated, but still the object of suspicion. However, he is now also part of the mainstream. He is a designer who has had the opportunity to pursue his aims to their logical conclusion. When he began to draw the strip cartoons 15 years ago in the cafés of the Barrio Gótico, he was subverting and parodying the form. His characters sprawled across the strips in the way that Dick Tracy and Superman did. But they were hardly superheroes, nor were they able to match the powerful impact of "real" strip cartoons with their coarse printing screens. Instead, Mariscal counterfeited the look of the strips with his pen in the same way that a skilled artist can fake the cross-hatching of a banknote.

The essence of Mariscal's early strip characters was that they were tongue-in-cheek. They filtered the form of genuine popular culture through inverted commas, but they weren't really part of it. Mariscal's strips were never read by the mainstream audience for the comic; they were comics metamorphosed for the avant-garde. What the Olympics have done is to present Mariscal's work, no longer simply as a quotation that distanced itself from the originals on which it was based, but rather as a genuine piece of the popular vernacular, reproduced as endlessly, and therefore both as mundanely and as powerfully as a Coke bottle, or Popeye. It's a trick that many have attempted, but few have carried off successfully. In the past, Olympic mascots have aspired to the genuinely common touch – to create popular images. However, all previous attempts failed to achieve this, and were for the most part content to rely on the patronising and cynical recycling of over-used imagery. Mariscal by contrast has taken a bold leap in a different direction. Cobi is not a self-conscious attempt to re-invent Mickey Mouse or Donald Duck by apeing the forms of Disney, an exercise doomed to failure. Rather, like Disney before him, Mariscal has used his personal vision to create an image with extraordinary power.

The danger for Mariscal is the way in which the very banality of the Cobi image threatens to exhaust his material. The hundreds of characters that his studio has churned out to feed the voracious

A silk scarf designed for COOB'92 and produced by Richel

appetite of the Olympic signage programme have assumed the scale of a moderately sized industry. And while Cobi may look pretty convincing as a swimmer, or a tennis player, or even a baseball player, there was always the possibility that by the time that Mariscal came up with Cobi in the guise of a modern pentathlete or a hockey player, he would run out of steam. For his figures to work as the identity for the games, they must all charm. There is no room for treading water with them – it's a high-risk strategy. By contrast, no one expected charm from the pictograms that Otl Aicher had devised with sober thoroughness for the Munich Olympics; they were meant to be an exercise in cool logic. The Mariscal programme will only be as strong as its weakest part. By contrast, the Aicher approach, which is to say the conventional graphic designer's approach, can take a more relaxed attitude, retreating into the anonymity of its graphic uniform.

Mariscal, on the other hand, is offering "art" which depends on maintaining the same level of invention throughout the whole programme. This is a demand that Mariscal is fully prepared to face. He sees the direct simplicity of his early work as having been forced on him by expediency. He is using the opportunity presented by the enormous volume of Olympics-related work to explore some of the techniques that have always interested him. Film was always a preoccupation of his, and appropriately Cobi will star in a 26-part animated TV series. Computers have turned Cobi into a 3-dimensional character roaming around Barcelona with a cast of characters that includes a couple of villains: Dr Normal and Don Tamino, who are pitted against Cobi and his friends Jordi, Cachas, Olivia, Nosi, Petra and Bicho. The scripts were written by El Tricicle, a Barcelona theatre company, and animated by the Madrid-based production company BRB, and once more gave Mariscal the scope to take his ideas further. While he has abdicated responsibility for any attempt to control all the applications of Cobi being auctioned off to the highest bidder by the marketing arm of the Olympic Committee, he did build on the experience to create special incarnations of Cobi for the major Olympic

Images from the Official Cobi manual, produced in 1988 by Mariscal in collaboration with Josep María Trias's studio Quod Disseny. Cobi was an inescapable presence in Barcelona long before the games themselves got underway

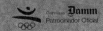 SETEMBRE OCTUBRE

						1
2	3	4	5	6	7	8
9	10	11	12	13	14	15
16	17	18	19	20	21	22
23/30	24	25	26	27	28	29

1	2	3	4	5	6
7	8	9	10	11	12	13
14	15	16	17	18	19	20
21	22	23	24	25	26	27
28	29	30	31			

The older Barcelona of
Gaudí filtered through
Mariscal's drawing –
from the 1991 calendar
produced by the Spanish
brewing company Damm

sponsors, which include IBM, Xerox, Coca-Cola and Kodak.

Mariscal is already moving on to projects that have the same breadth as the Olympics. In Japan he has been involved in various large-scale projects in connection with the new high-speed railway lines. These projects encompass a range of applications from architecture – in collaboration with Alfredo Arribas – to uniforms.

The Olympics will be a major watershed in Mariscal's career. He has left his counter-cultural past behind him and is now getting the chance to work on larger- and larger-scale projects, with bigger budgets and more elaborate briefs. The signs are that he has the resources, and the ability, to move rapidly into a much wider view of design.

In an age when ideas are in short supply, but in increasing demand by industry of all kinds, Mariscal has a very strong personal vision of what design can offer. He has the ideas, and he also has the ability to work with a range of specialised designers – architects such as Alfredo Arribas, and furniture designers such as Pepe Cortés for example – to turn those ideas into commercial projects. In the process, Mariscal has made a major contribution toward redefining not only the character of design, but also the working methods of design as well. Mariscal's relationship with Arribas, typically, is completely out of the normal run of collaborations. It is not just the connection between the designer and the enabler. Rather, it is a genuine collaboration between two highly creative individuals who confront a problem from two very different directions. For Andrea Branzi, who in 1991 staged a major exhibition of European design at the Centre Pompidou in Paris, along with Paris and Milan, Barcelona was one of the major centres. It was a city that embodied what Branzi saw as the New Design, a resolution of the contradictions and paradoxes that characterise post-industrial culture. This is a view of design that stresses its emotional content, one which juxtaposes high-tech and low-tech, mass production and one-offs, ephemera and permanence. It's a definition that could be said to characterise Mariscal himself.

Exhibitions

1976
- Galería Magic, Barcelona. *The Veo*

1977
- Galería Mec-Mec, Barcelona. *Gran Hotel* (comics, drawings, glass paintings, sculpture, videos and montage)*

1978
- Detrás-Vinçon, Barcelona. *Decorapart* (glass paintings and montage)*

1979
- Galeries Eude, Gaspar, Ciento, Joan Prats and BCD, Barcelona. *Festa de la Lletra*

1980
- Galería Central and Galería Local, Madrid (drawings, montage of restored furniture and fabrics)*

1981
- Palau de la Virreina, Barcelona. *Homenatge a Picasso*
- Sala Vinçon, Barcelona. *Muebles Amorales* (furniture prototypes)*

*One man exhibition

1982
- Galería 13, Barcelona. *Montaje Acción 3RL* (performance)*
- Galería Fúcares, Almagro, Ciudad Real, Spain. (drawings)*
- Sala Vinçon, Barcelona. *Marieta* (montage with Marieta fabrics)*
- Pabellones de Arte, Barcelona. *Barcelona Vuit - Dos*
- Banco Exterior de España, Barcelona. *Cataluña Vista desde el Exterior*
- Grandson & Grandson, Madrid. *Ven a Verte*
- Galería René Metrás, Barcelona. *Ceesepe, Ouka Lele, Hortelano, Mariscal*
- Memphis, International Style, Milan. (travelling exhibition organised in Milan and promoted by Memphis)

1983
- B.D Ediciones de Diseño, Barcelona. *Muebles Muy Formales* (furniture designed in collabration with Pepe Cortés)*
- Galería Roca, Sabadell (Barcelona). (drawings)*
- Librería Look, Barcelona. *Supermercat*
- Galería Moriarty, Madrid (drawings and glass paintings)*
- Galería Temple, Valencia (glass paintings and drawings)*
- Philadelphia Museum of Art, Philadelphia. *Design since 1945*
- La Caixa, Barcelona. *Blauhaus*
- Galería René Metrás, Barcelona. *Retratos Finales Siglo XX*

1984
- *Espace Actuel*, Paris. (drawings, graphic work and products)*
- *Exposicion Itinerante El Víbora*, Barcelona (travelling exhibition)
- *Phoenix, International Exhibition of New Design Works*, Toronto
- Fundació Joan Miró, Barcelona. *Tintín a Barcelona, Homenatge a Hergé* (travelling exhibition)
- *T-Shirt Show*, Milan. (travelling exhibition)
- La Caixa, Barcelona. *84 x 20, Un Maremàgnum Gráfic* (travelling exhibition)

1985

● Galería Luís Adelantado, Valencia. *Tres Sofás* (prototypes of furniture)*
● Studio Totem, Lyon (paintings and products)*
● Galería Moriarty-Arco '85, Madrid (paintings)
● Museo de Arte Moderno, Madrid. *Proyectos Inéditos de Diseño Español.* Sponsor: Artespaña
● Galería Rafael Ortiz, Seville. *Postales*
● Galería Moriarty, Madrid. *Las Ciudades*
● Europalia, Brussels. *Diseño en España*
● Ajuntament de Barcelona. *BCN 10 x 12. 10 Districtes, 12 Il.lustradors*
● *8 Diseñadores en Color Core* (travelling exhibition). Sponsor: Fórmica

1986

● Galería Molí Casals, Calonge, Gerona, Spain (paintings)*
● Galería Carlos Sicart, Cadaqués, Gerona, Spain (paintings)*
● Galería Rafael Ortiz, Seville (paintings)*
● Sala Vinçon, Barcelona. *Esculturas Adelantadas en el Nuevo Estilo Post-Barroco* (sculpture)*
● Galería Moriarty-Arco '86, Madrid
● D. Barcelona, Barcelona. *Paraguas Inmorales*
● Espace MCC, St. Etienne, France. *Barcelone*

1987

● Galería Moriarty, Madrid. (paintings)*
● *Dokumenta 8*, Kassel, Germany
● Centre Georges Pompidou, Paris. *Les Avant-gardes de la Fin du XX Siècle*

1988

● Fundació BCD, Barcelona. *Design in Catalonia* (travelling exhibition)
● La Lonja, Valencia. *100 Años con Mariscal* (anthology)*

1989

● Galería Eude, Barcelona. (engravings)*
● Galería Berini, Barcelona. (oil paintings)*
● Galería Moriarty-Arco '89, Madrid (oil paintings)*
● Buque Rey Favila, Moll de la Fusta, Barcelona. *Cent Anys a Bar Cel Ona* (anthology, Barcelona's version of the exhibition *100 Anys con Mariscal*)*
● Sala Vinçon, Barcelona. *Cosquillas para tus Ojos* (sculpture)*
● Galería Trayecto, Vitoria. (watercolours on rice-paper)*

1990

● The Armory, New York. *Catalonia-New York*
● Galería Moriarty-Arco '90, Madrid (sculpture)
● Galería Luís Adelantado, Valencia (watercolours on rice-paper)*
● *La Otra Cara de la Acuarela*, Valencia (travelling exhibition)
● Galería Moriarty, Madrid (paintings, glass paintings)*
● Galería Berini, Barcelona. *Cristalografías* (glass paintings)*

1991

● Centre Georges Pompidou, Paris. *Les Capitales Européenes du Nouveau Design*
● *Cartells Espanyols d'Utilitat Pública*, Barcelona
● Salón Internacional del Cómic, Barcelona. *S.O.S. Racisme*

Bibliography

Neón de Suro. Published by Editora Balear, Palma de Mallorca, 1976

Apuntes de Garriris. Published by J. Mariscal, Barcelona, 1977, for the exhibition Gran Hotel

Metrópolis. Published by J. Mariscal, Barcelona, 1977, for the exhibition Gran Hotel

ABCDari Il.lustrat. Published by A. Bosch, Editor, Barcelona, 1978

Fuego en las Entrañas. Published by Editorial La Cúpula, Barcelona, 1981. Story by Pedro Almodóvar, illustrations by J. Mariscal

Mariscal. Published by Le Dernier Terrain Vague, Paris, 1983. Authors: Lionel Hoebeke and Jean Seisser

Agenda Mariscal. Published by Àmbit Serveis Editorials, Barcelona, 1984. Author: Llátzer Moix

De Diseño , no. 10 (special monograph edition dedicated to J. Mariscal). Published by El Croquis Editorial, Madrid, 1986. Directors: Juli Capella and Quim Larrea

Historias de Garriris. Published by Editorial Complot, Barcelona, 1987

100 Años con Mariscal. Published by IMPIVA – Instituto de la Mediana y Pequeña Industria de la Generalitat Valenciana, Valencia, 1988

Graphic Poster I. Published by Productos Compactos, Barcelona, 1988

Graphic Poster II. Published by Productos Compactos, Barcelona, 1989

Cent Anys a BAR CEL ONA. Published by J. Mariscal, Barcelona, 1989. (A re-publication of the catalogue *100 Anyos con Mariscal* for the exhibition Cent Anys a BAR CEL ONA, Mariscal published by the Galería Trayecto, Vitoria, 1989

J. Mariscal. Catalogue published by the Galería Trayecto, Vitoria, 1989

J. Mariscal. Catalogue published by the Galería Luís Adelantado, Valencia, 1990